War and Negative Revelation

War and Negative Revelation

A Theoethical Reflection on Moral Injury

Michael S. Yandell

LEXINGTON BOOKS
Lanham • Boulder • New York • London

Published by Lexington Books
An imprint of The Rowman & Littlefield Publishing Group, Inc.
4501 Forbes Boulevard, Suite 200, Lanham, Maryland 20706
www.rowman.com

86-90 Paul Street, London EC2A 4NE

Copyright © 2022 by The Rowman & Littlefield Publishing Group, Inc.

All rights reserved. No part of this book may be reproduced in any form or by any electronic or mechanical means, including information storage and retrieval systems, without written permission from the publisher, except by a reviewer who may quote passages in a review.

British Library Cataloguing in Publication Information Available

Library of Congress Cataloging-in-Publication Data

Names: Yandell, Michael S., 1984- author.
Title: War and negative revelation : a theoethical reflection on moral injury / Michael S. Yandell.
Description: Lanham : Lexington Books, [2022] | Includes bibliographical references and index.
Identifiers: LCCN 2022001777 (print) | LCCN 2022001778 (ebook) | ISBN 9781793641922 (cloth) | ISBN 9781793641946 (paperback) | ISBN 9781793641939 (epub)
Subjects: LCSH: War—Moral and ethical aspects. | Moral injuries. | War—Religious aspects. | Revelation.
Classification: LCC U22 .Y36 2022 (print) | LCC U22 (ebook) | DDC 172/.42—dc23/eng/20220208
LC record available at https://lccn.loc.gov/2022001777
LC ebook record available at https://lccn.loc.gov/2022001778

This work is dedicated to Amy, my partner in everything.

Contents

Preface	ix
Acknowledgments	xiii
Introduction	1
1 Anti-life: The Logic of War	13
2 Domination as Freedom: Anti-life and Global War	35
3 Moral Injury as Negative Revelation, Part I: "Moral"—Betrayed by Convention	57
4 Moral Injury as Negative Revelation, Part II: "Injury"—Loss of Meaning	77
5 Negative Revelation and Turning to Life	97
References	121
Index	127
About the Author	131

Preface

I wrote this book with a heavy heart, at times hearing the echo of an old Army cadence: "somebody ain't goin' make it, cause their puny little heart can't take it."[1] I have wanted to tell a truth about war for some time now. I have also wanted to avoid truth-telling about war. I went to war in 2004, as a young enlisted soldier in the U.S. Army. That same year, I returned home. Sixteen years have passed since I set foot back in the United States after six months in Iraq. The truth is, no matter how much time has passed, I am still viscerally angry about the war; and, because I participated in it, I am viscerally angry with myself. The war makes me angry, and so I wish to tell the truth about it. The war that makes me angry is also a part of me, and so I wish to pretend that it does not exist. My heart can't take it.

I was heavily armed when I went to war. My least potent weapon was my rifle. I carried the passion of youth and a feeling of invulnerability. I drank from a bottomless well of righteous indignation, a well that was constantly replenished with replayed footage of the World Trade Center burning and collapsing. My thinking took the shape of patriotic ideals that could be expressed as talking points, or, when words failed, could be summoned in the image of the American flag. Those ideals were protected by a thick armor of youthful naiveté. My most reliable weapon was a deep-seated, seemingly unshakable, faith in God. I did not understand this God in whom I had faith, but I was certain that this God was on my side and that I was on God's side. I went to war with the blunt instrument of certainty that I was doing God's will.

By the time I was medically discharged from the Army in 2006, all my weapons were gone. The rifle was locked safely in an arms room and is the only weapon I carried that (I assume) still functions. My passion turned to cold-hearted cynicism. My feeling of invulnerability was shaken through war and was finally stamped out by my being deemed unfit for duty. My well ran dry of both righteousness and indignation. My thinking took the shape of guilt and shame that no wealth of talking points could ever articulate; the flag that had once prompted me to stand proudly at attention now compelled me to cast my eyes downward. As for certainty regarding God, it was at this point in my life that I was perhaps closer to the truth than I had ever been before: God's will had become an unfathomable mystery, something that I could not connect in any meaningful way to my service in war.

What is one to do when one's way of making sense of the world crumbles? For about a year-long period before I was discharged, I was stuck trying to decide between two abysmal prospects: to take my own life or to somehow begin to live day to day in a world that no longer made sense to me. I am grateful to still count myself among the living; life has offered up surprises I could never have imagined in that period in which I was stuck. It was no strength of will on my own part that kept me breathing; I was fortunate to be surrounded by good people—people who remained good to me when I was not good to be around. Their care and attention were lifelines to me, lines that lashed me to life when I wanted nothing to do with it. Life continues for me.

Why this baring of myself in a preface? Because without these experiences, there would be no preface, no book. People speak of hitting "rock-bottom" in many different contexts. I vividly remember my rock-bottom: the once squared-away soldier lying sedated and restrained on a hospital bed in a small psychiatric ward. My weapons were all gone.

All that I am now is a surprise because I could not imagine then any possible outcome of a meaningful life. I did not have hope, which I understand as the capacity to imagine a different set of circumstances. I despaired of life; the future seemed narrow and foreclosed. To connect my life now to that moment can only be described by grace; I eventually became open to that grace and flourished. Because I had superiors that cared about their soldiers, I left the Army with a medical retirement rather than disgrace. My goal then was to get far away from the Army and the war and not look back. The farthest distance from the Army and the war that I could manage in a short time was returning home and pursuing a degree in music education with the help of the G.I. Bill. This suited my goal, and I began to be able to visualize myself as a music teacher in a small town somewhere with a comfortable life—a life of grace.

The truth is that I was, and I am still, angry about the war. I have yet to settle down as a music teacher in a small town; instead, I pursued theological education and ordination into Christian ministry. My weapons were all gone, but memories of war and memories of faith in God remained. These memories presented themselves to me, often unbidden. War and God left their marks on me, and I needed to make sense of them. I ended up here: a scholar, a minister, needing to write some truth about war.

I am still angry about the war. I want to tell the truth about it, as much as I can, and I also want to hide from the truth. The temptation to shy away from the truth presents itself at every turn. As I try to make sense of things, it is tempting to speak of a transcendent God, a God beyond and above any war here on earth—a God untouched by my experience of war. However, I fear that I would then have a God that leaves me untouchable, and I long for the touch of God. It is also tempting to write about war and God in a scholarly voice that brackets my own experience. Indeed, many would encourage such an approach. Yet without the experience, there would be no voice and nothing to say.

I try to remember when I was at the depth of despair, years ago now. All of this is a grace. I have nothing to lose with this venture, and all to gain. The baring of myself in this preface serves as my reminder that the desire that brought me to this place in which I have the luxury to write is the desire to try and tell the truth about war and of God, as best as I am able to tell it. I want to tell it, because as I sit with these thoughts, these books, and these words on my computer screen, I do not sit alone. These memories of war are also memories of people, and I will not be so afraid of the truth that I forget them. That means I am present in the work, as a human being and as a scholar, because they are present to me. I am present as one who desperately wants to hold on to something true and good, because I know and have known truly good people. For all our sakes, I want to tell the truth about war and God, even if I can only "tell it slant."[2] I want to shy away from this project, but I think I'll make it; I think my heart can take it.

NOTES

1. An Army running cadence I heard one morning at Fort Hood, TX. https://www.armystudyguide.com/content/cadence/running_cadence/the-motivator.shtml

2. Emily Dickinson. "Tell All the Truth, But Tell It Slant," 1868, in *Poetry: A Pocket Anthology*, 5th edition, ed. R. S Gwynn (New York: Pearson/Longman, 2007), 179.

Acknowledgments

Ed Waggoner and Rita Nakashima Brock encouraged me to pursue a PhD in theology. Beyond encouragement, they have mentored me, influenced my thinking, and have given me the gift of numerous insightful conversations over the years on a variety of subjects. I am most grateful for the many ways they have welcomed me into this field.

Faculty and students at Brite Divinity School, and friends at University Christian Church of Fort Worth, TX, provided an unrivaled network of support as I took my first steps in theological speaking and writing.

Friends and colleagues at Emory University have continued to offer such support. I especially thank my dissertation committee: Wendy Farley, Pamela Hall, Elizabeth Bounds, and Ellen Ott Marshall. They have each helped me find my voice and encouraged me to speak.

It was a joy and privilege to learn how to teach theology alongside Noel Erskine, and I also thank Dr. Erskine for sharing with me his passion for Dietrich Bonhoeffer. Joy McDougall and Kendall Soulen helped me avoid the error of disregarding Barth. Tara Doyle and Bobbi Patterson led by example in pedagogical excellence.

The women in the theological studies program at Arrendale State Prison influenced my thinking and kept me motivated more than they know. I thank Elizabeth Bounds and Rachelle Green for countless carpool conversations on the ways to and from Arrendale, and for teaching me what collegiality is.

Discourse regarding moral injury and trauma has been expanding at a rapid pace. It has been my privilege to learn in conversation with many scholars and practitioners over the years on this topic—a non-exhaustive list: Rita Nakashima Brock, Christina Conroy, Carrie Doehring, Kyle Fauntleroy, Gabriella Lettini, Joe McDonald, Joshua Morris, Zachary Moon, Shelly Rambo, Nancy Ramsay, and Joseph Wiinikka-Lydon. Thank you all.

Thank you to the women and men of the 752nd Ordnance Company (EOD), for helping me come back to life.

Thank you to First Christian Church (Disciples of Christ), Union City, Tennessee, for forming me in the faith.

My parents, Jane and John Yandell, my sister Arrah Ford: thank you for a lifetime of love and support. Thank you to Carolyn Derrick Parks, for offering her home as a writing retreat and for sundry gifts. My cousin Rebecca Stephens listened graciously as I obsessed over Donald Rumsfeld.

My partner in life, Amy Yandell, pierces the veil of anti-life each day. I dedicate this work to her.

Introduction

On the eve of the United States' global war on terror, George W. Bush opened his 9/11/2001 speech stating, "thousands of lives were suddenly ended by evil, despicable acts of terror" and he closed claiming that "we go forward to defend freedom and all that is good and just in our world."[1] These words name well my youthful exuberance at joining the Army, and my initial enthusiasm for going to Iraq as part of Operation Iraqi Freedom II. Defending goodness and justice in the world is a worthy enterprise. Now, twenty years later, C. J. Chivers describes the dissonance many of us feel as he writes of veterans of recent American wars: "These veterans confront something pernicious but usually invisible: the difficulties of trying to square their feelings of commitment after the terrorist attacks in 2001 with the knowledge that their lives were harnessed to wars that ran far past the pursuit of justice and ultimately did not succeed."[2] The commitment runs deep and so does the difficult knowledge.

To reframe Chivers's observation in my own words: these veterans committed themselves to the pursuit and defense of goodness and justice, and in the concrete situation of war they found that goodness and justice are absent. Something does not add up. It is a central claim of this book that it is not the level of commitment to ideals and values, such as goodness and justice, that results in the difficulty veterans have squaring their feelings and knowledge; rather, it is that the values themselves have already been twisted out of shape and made into means to serve other ends. Put another way, making a commitment to pursue justice is valuable, but the value of justice has been structured in such a way that the one committing to pursue it is deceived. To continue using George W. Bush's remarks as a point of departure, something that does not square in war is "what is good and just in our world"; as Chivers states, the war went beyond "the pursuit of justice." In Bush's speech, "good" and "just" seem synonymous, but the U.S. warfighter and those against whom they fight learn a different lesson.

According to Origen, an ancient Christian theologian, goodness and justice *should* be considered synonymously: "if a virtue is something good, and justice is a virtue, undoubtedly justice is goodness"; Origen goes on to say, "as we call evil and injustice one and the same wickedness, we should hold goodness and justice to be one and the same virtue."[3] Origen was arguing with other ancient thinkers who distinguished goodness from justice; in his view, they misunderstood the concepts: "For they think that justice is to do evil to the evil and good to the good; that is, according to their meaning, that one who is just will not show himself well disposed to the evil, but will behave towards them with a kind of hatred."[4] This theme of the interrelatedness of goodness and justice will recur throughout this book. Justice *is* goodness or a mode of goodness. If we come to realize that our works of "justice" in the world are actually driven by a "kind of hatred," any claim we have on doing what is good will also be forfeit. For Origen, and for my project, goodness and justice are concrete relational realities, not abstract concepts. They are shown to be relational in the work of Origen, as his argument against his opponents is centered on how God and human beings *behave toward* other people. Goodness and justice as relational realities will be taken up more thoroughly in chapter 5 in dialogue with Emmanuel Lévinas and Dietrich Bonhoeffer.

There is a long-standing tradition of just war theory that rules out "a kind of hatred" in war-fighting; in fact, soldiers on both sides of a conflict should be treated as "moral equals."[5] However, what Chivers observes holds true: veterans face a difficulty squaring "their feelings of commitment . . . with the knowledge that their lives were harnessed to wars that ran far past the pursuit of justice."[6] Much of this work will be toward elucidating "a kind of hatred" in twenty-first century U.S. war-waging, and fleshing out what is obscured and covered over when politicians allude to goodness and justice. "A kind of hatred" may not be the best description of that which masquerades underneath the cover of goodness and justice; greed, fear, anxiety, and insecurity may end up proving to be better descriptors. In the first chapter, I will lay out a concept of "anti-life" that entails a hatred for life. The immediate problem of the experience of war however, to put it simply, is that many of us wanted to *be* good by *doing* what is just; we found that we were doing something unjust—now, what does that make us? What does that make of the "goodness and justice" we set out to defend?

THESIS

The central claim I am developing throughout this book is that the experience of war can be a revelatory experience. However, the revelation of war is not the disclosure of some previously unknown positive content. I am offering a phenomenology of "negative revelation" in which false or distorted claims of goodness and justice disintegrate, becoming meaningless in the concrete experience of war. This disintegration of meaning is itself a meaningful experience, "revealing" here comes to signify the presence of goodness and justice through the profound experience of their *absence*.[7] War's revelation includes the awareness and mourning that goodness and justice were wrongly conceived, with a simultaneous longing for a genuine goodness and justice of which one is no longer certain but for which one hopes. This negative revelation is a turning from an old "justice" that was a kind of hatred, toward something new that is yet unknown. One does not mourn the loss of toxic goodness and justice and long to be poisoned again; rather, one finds that one has always been thirsting for an antidote.

In chapter 4 of this book, I offer a phenomenology of the disintegration of meaning, through a side-by-side reading of Alasdair MacIntyre and Susan Brison. For MacIntyre, a sense of *telos*—an orientation toward an ultimate good or end—is essential for the intelligibility of a "self." Brison shows how trauma disrupts and destroys a sense of such an intelligible *telos*. My attempt throughout the book is to demonstrate a perverse structuring of goodness and justice in the way the United States organized and executed the global war on terror in response to the events of 9/11/2001. Many individuals fought the war convinced that their efforts were oriented toward a grand *telos*—a work of goodness and justice for the world—only to find their lives were oriented to something resembling a kind of hatred.

War is an experience in which a person sets out confident she is doing good, because a priori—or before the reality of war—she is confident that she is good or on the side of the good. For such a person, the actuality of war may be a revelatory experience; real encounters with other people may dissolve her a priori sense of goodness into meaninglessness. Rita Nakashima Brock and Gabriella Lettini frame this loss of meaning in their work on "moral injury," a concept which will be explored in detail in chapters 3 and 4 of this book: "Moral injury results when soldiers violate their core moral beliefs, and in evaluating their behavior negatively, they feel they no longer live in a reliable, meaningful world and can no longer be regarded as decent human beings."[8] By witnessing and/or participating in a kind of hatred for the other (i.e., by seeing the way the enterprise of war diminishes, reduces, and objectifies the other), one is stripped of the confidence that one is doing good, and her being good may also be called into question, creating an existential crisis. Paul Tillich points to this link between "being" and "doing" by combining ontology and ethics in the concept of "courage," the "ethical act in which man affirms his own being in spite of those elements of his existence which conflict with his essential self-affirmation."[9] The other side of this revelation is an apophatic knowledge of goodness: goodness is known through its absence or by realizing that goodness is not here. To experience the absence of goodness is still to perceive the good and to long for it.[10]

For the past several years, I have been part of several ongoing conversations around the concept of "moral injury," a term that has rapidly gained attention and a wealth of literature over the past twenty years. Chapters 3 and 4 of this book deal directly with some of that literature. As a person who self-identifies as morally injured, while simultaneously being engaged in academic discussions on the topic, I have felt a growing dissatisfaction with the directions toward which the literature generally trends. At the heart of this project, I am adding an additional layer or depth to moral injury as a "negative revelation." My dissatisfaction with the literature is that conversations about moral injury often tend to focus on individuals and individual actions/events that take place during war. I am claiming, throughout this work, that "morality" has been compromised long before specific events occur on battlefields. I am paying close attention to the context of war itself and specific attention to the war the United States has been waging since 9/11/2001. The logic of our global war on terror has stolen something from human life, and I develop moral injury as a recognition of this theft. It is important to note: I am not saying something entirely new with my dissatisfaction with the term "moral injury"; others have raised similar concerns (see chapter 3 and 4). I also do not seek to *replace* working definitions of moral injury with my own. However, I do hope to provide, in the pages that follow, a unique angle and layer of complexity.

METHOD

The late Marcella Althaus-Reid reminds us of the "old premise of Liberation Theology": "first comes reality; theology is only a second act"; she goes on to say "however, what has not been clearly thought out is how reality is conformed; what is excluded and what is included in that definition of reality needs a more thoughtful reflection."[11] Althaus-Reid's aim was to illuminate how complex oppression really is, beyond how early liberation theologians dealt with it. She demonstrated how sexuality and poverty combined to form multifaceted oppressions, especially in her home of Buenos Aires.[12] Her targets were "decency and order," and how those ideological constructs had cast out from reality what was really real in the lives of people—labeling them "indecent" and disordered.[13]

To be sure, no one has a clear grasp of "reality" first to then move to reflection, theological or otherwise, as a second act. "Reality" is always shaped and formed by the way thinking subjects perceive reality and are already reflecting on it. Althaus-Reid's attention to "how reality is conformed" does not throw out reflection for the sake of action, but demands that thinkers also reflect on reflection itself—how do reflections that give rise to ideology already profoundly shape the "reality" in which real human bodies interact? Althaus-Reid showed how liberation theology was able to illuminate and resist deceptions about poverty but left the ideological deceptions of patriarchy and heterosexual normativity relatively untouched.

In this book, I am aiming to illuminate how deceptions surrounding war function in a manner that in some ways parallel Althaus-Reid's insights—how the physical carnage of war is already largely seen as problematic, while ideological deceptions that lead to such carnage are left relatively untouched. The content of my project is quite different than Althaus-Reid's, though there is a methodological element of "indecenting" working implicitly throughout, a process Althaus-Reid describes as "coming back to the authentic, everyday life experiences described as odd by the ideology—and mythology—makers alike. Indecenting brings back the sense of reality."[14] A nation cannot go to war, I argue, without the aid of ideology and mythology makers. War's revelation is the destruction and disintegration of ideologies and mythologies. It leaves a void of goodness and justice, and whatever goodness and justice may come to fill that void cannot take the shape of ideological certainty.

My project has two primary foci: war and revelation. Both have to do primarily with reality, and secondarily with theology—though again, reality is already profoundly shaped by theories and theologies. My own personal reality of war is partially disclosed in the preface, and it will surface occasionally throughout this book. H. Richard Niebuhr warns: "the great source of evil in life is the absolutizing of the relative."[15] He is certainly not alone among theologians in raising this caution. For that reason, I will be mindful not to rely too heavily on my own personal experience of war as a source for this book. Nevertheless, my own experience will of course serve in the background as a kind of compass and motivation for my work; I cannot pretend to be unbiased. Also, my experience was the first disruption in my own patterns of thinking shaped by the absolutization of relatives. A presupposition and assumption undergirding this entire book is that war is one of the greatest sources of human suffering—in terms of both intensity and quantity—in our world, and it should therefore be regarded as one of the world's greatest evils.

There is and always will be debate regarding the possible necessity of warfare, but regardless of necessity there is always an element of human intentionality in war. Wars are *intended* and *chosen* by people, no matter how constrained by circumstance and emergency people may be. I do argue that my presupposition of war as one of the greatest evils is part of the revelatory event of war itself. However, because this now functions as my presupposition, I must be even more alert to the danger of absolutizing that relative observation.

This book is not an attempt to show that the use of coercive force in a situation of emergency is inherently evil; I am also uninterested in demonstrating that the use of force can ever be good. I am focusing specifically on the global war on terror waged by the United States in the twenty-first century, especially the invasion and occupation of Iraq. It is this specific, concrete example of war and its consequences that drive my argument about war and negative revelation. Nevertheless, there is a broader implication of this book about the project of war in general—especially war utilizing all the devastating power that twenty-first century technologies have to offer. The broader implication or speculation is that the use of coercive force in the situation of emergency (and the process of defining "emergency" itself) is always dangerously susceptible to deceptive erosions and a toxic structuring of goodness and justice—to the point that goodness is no longer recognized as such.

The form of this book follows a kind of dynamic arc, from theoretical concepts to the concreteness of human life. I wish to follow Althaus-Reid's admonishment to prioritize reality with theology as a second act. However, to also think through how reality is conformed, I begin with a theory of the logic of war, what I call "anti-life." That anti-life comes first in the order of chapters should not be taken to mean that I grant it primacy. Rather, I am trying to elucidate how the concrete situation of global war has become a reality by beginning with its logical and theoretical roots. In the dynamic between universal and particular, I am taking cues from H. Richard Niebuhr, who accepted and acknowledged the limit of "historical relativism": "What has made the question about revelation a contemporary and pressing question for Christians is the realization that the point of view which a [person] occupies in regarding religious as well as any other sort of reality is of profound importance."[16] In speaking of the universal or the general, one always speaks from a particular point of view. Acknowledging this limit, for Niebuhr, does not imply that one cannot access the truth at all: "Relativism does not imply subjectivism and skepticism. It is not evident that the man who is forced to confess that his view of things is conditioned by the standpoint he occupies must doubt the reality of what he sees."[17] It is with this limit of a particular point of view that can never be absolutized, combined with the hope that something true can be seen from a particular point of view, that I set out to attempt to tell a "truth" about war, through what the experience of war itself reveals. I tell "a" truth here, acknowledging that with truth there is multiplicity. When I claim to tell the truth, I am trying to draw attention to something I believe is true that is often obscured. I am not claiming to possess "The Truth." Such an absolute claim to truth is, in fact, the injustice I am railing against in the pages that follow. The United States' global war in the twenty-first century has claimed truth for itself, robbing humanity of the right to speak for itself.

The sources I use to elucidate war and its revelation are quite varied. Theological and philosophical sources will be used to develop a phenomenology of negative revelation and to describe the logic of war. Recalling Althaus-Reid's language, there is much ideology and mythology built into the project of the global war on terror. There is a thick set of narratives, traditions, and practices that shape the formulation of that to which U.S. warfighters are oriented as *telos* or ultimate aim—"defending what is good and just in our world." I use theology and philosophy to critique and attempt to cut through this mythology, to show how what is good and just in the lives of real human beings has been obscured and redefined by a U.S.-led effort of domination. For the reality of war itself, I draw on testimonies and stories about war. Some of these testimonies are the recounting of events that really happened to real people. Some of the literature from which I will draw is fictional, though a "real" representation of war in a different way. All of these reflect particular points of view and say something true about war, though never "The Truth." While these points of view illuminate different aspects of war itself, they all deal with revelation in the experience of war.

It is important to note why I include fiction and why I consider it a vitally important source. The first reason is provided by Tim O'Brien, who distinguishes between "story-truth" and "happening-truth":

> I want you to feel what I felt. I want you to know why story-truth is truer sometimes than happening-truth.
>
> Here is the happening-truth. I was once a soldier. There were many bodies, real bodies with real faces, but I was young then and I was afraid to look. And now, twenty years later, I'm left with faceless responsibility and faceless grief.
>
> Here is the story-truth. He was a slim, dead, almost dainty young man of about twenty. He lay in the center of a red clay trail near the village of My Khe. His jaw was in his throat. His one eye was shut, the other eye was a star-shaped hole. I killed him.
>
> What stories can do, I guess is make things present. I can look at things I never looked at. I can attach faces to grief and love and pity and God. I can be brave. I can make myself feel again.[18]

"Story-truths" are vitally important to truth-telling about war. They are not lies about "happening-truth," but they bring something to light about what happened that cannot be disclosed in a list of chronological facts. The "story-truth" of the claim, "I killed him," in the passage discloses the truth of being linked to death whether one killed someone or not. O'Brien writes: "I was present, you see, and my presence was guilt enough. . . . I remember feeling the burden of responsibility and grief."[19] Certain realities, such as the reality of responsibility and grief, can sometimes best be captured in "story-truth."

Martha Nussbaum provides the second rationale in turning to fiction, in her analysis of a novel (Henry James's *Golden Bowl*) for a source of moral philosophy rather than a "real" life:

> When we examine our own lives, we have so many obstacles to correct vision, so many motives to blindness and stupidity. The "vulgar heat" of jealousy and personal interest comes between us and the loving perception of each particular. A novel, just because it is not our life, places us in a moral position that is favorable for perception and it shows us what it would be like to take up that position in life.[20]

We may not be able to transcend or escape from our particular points of view, but literature can provide for a certain perception of *depth*; we perceive moral truth more clearly simply because the moral truth is not so obscured by our own life processes. Literature, in my reading of Nussbaum, occupies a certain middle ground or mediating relationship between general philosophical concepts and a real and concrete human life. Aristotelian moral philosophy utilizes "critical and distinction-making skills" to provide a humble "outline" or "sketch" of the "salient features of our moral life."[21] These critical skills for making distinctions are vital for a richer understanding of morality, as are the sketches and outlines; however, the "outline" of moral life that philosophy provides needs *life* for its actual content.[22] Nussbaum, in the spirit of Henry James, wants philosophy to be in alliance with literature.

When I draw on fictional literature in this project, I do so both for the depth such literature provides in getting at "story-truths" of war and also to deal with life in the relatively safe space of a story. To put it another way, I do not wish to exploit human suffering for my own project. Althaus-Reid observes: "Over the dead bodies, the bodies of people who suffered and felt their life to be sometimes intolerable, theology was written."[23] I have seen and heard too many politicians and pundits stuff words into the mouths of people killed in war to forward a patriotic agenda. I will not stuff my own words into the mouths of the dead to counter that patriotic agenda. Literature does not completely transcend this problem, but the "life" (and the death) it makes present can be seen more clearly simply because it is not our own. Where I do draw on the real experiences of others, I use already published material, attempting to take great care in my reading of others' stories. Methodologically, this project is largely experiential. I use experiential and fictional narratives—all read through my own experiences. I acknowledge here my own positionality—that I cannot read accounts of war with my own experience of war divorced from the reading. I take care to make clear distinctions between my own experience and other sources from which I draw, though I am still making an interpretative move when drawing on stories that are not my own.

Finally, the "bookends" of my project—chapters 1 and 5—draw heavily from the particular point of view of Christian theology. Theology also deals with stories—or as Paul Tillich puts it—with "myths" as "symbols of faith combined in stories about divine-human encounters."[24] At this point it is sufficient to say that the United States also combines symbols into the myth of the American war story. Shelly Rambo states, "While there has been significant scholarship exposing the problem of the alliance between the Christian story and the American war story, there have been few attempts to reclaim the Christian story from the perspective of those who have been touched by war most closely."[25] Therefore, the last rationale for turning to stories and testimonies is to begin (only to begin) to disentangle the Christian story from the American war story.

CHAPTER OUTLINE

Chapter 1 is the most theoretical piece of this work, an analysis of the logic of war that I call "anti-life." My thesis in this whole project is that goodness and justice are "revealed" through their absence in war. The concept of anti-life is a radical negation of life—the negation of goodness and justice by reducing human beings to objects of fear, making life a thing, a threat, that can be manipulated and controlled through force. This reduction or diminishment of life itself is what I mean when I say that global war on terror has stolen something of humanity. Throughout the chapter, my primary interlocutors are Karl Barth, Paul Tillich, Hannah Arendt, and Dietrich Bonhoeffer. I draw on each of these thinkers to construct a step-by-step working definition of anti-life: *a static, parasitic, explanatory assault on the inexhaustible mystery of life.* In more down-to-earth language, anti-life poses as life and is a false authoritative claim on the good and the just. "Anti-life," as I develop it in chapter 1, is a concept that carries with it broader implications about the use of force beyond the global war on terror—how domination can take on the disguise of justice. After chapter 1, I apply anti-life with increasing specificity to the invasion and occupation of Iraq. The reader may wish to apply the concept of anti-life to any war that has gone beyond the pursuit of justice. For my purposes, I develop anti-life as a concept to point out the specific injustice of our current war, and how the global war on terror operates as a death-dealing deception.

Chapter 2 develops the concept of anti-life with a layer of specificity. Here I demonstrate that domination has posed as freedom in the logic of the global war on terror; this is anti-life in the twenty-first century. I emphasize three facets of domination in the guise of freedom in the global war on terror: "full spectrum dominance" (domination through military power), "American sovereignty" (domination through political power), and "good and evil" (domination through a pretense of moral superiority—ideological power). Throughout this chapter, former U.S. Secretary of Defense Donald Rumsfeld serves as a primary interlocutor.

An additional word on Rumsfeld: focusing on one architect/executor of the war helped me to give this decades spanning war some narrative focus in my argument. I am also, frankly, quite fascinated by Rumsfeld and his (in) famous public epistemological musings. The space dedicated to Rumsfeld in these pages should not be read as an implicit claim that I feel he is most responsible for the war or that he is more blameworthy than others in the Bush administration for its horrors. There are, I think, easier targets than Donald Rumsfeld; however, he *is* a responsible party, to be sure. While I find myself at odds with his actions and priorities (as best as I can reconstruct them here), it is my intention to treat his point of view in good faith.

Chapter 3 begins my dialogue with and contribution to the discourse on "moral injury." I provide a very brief review of the term through oft-cited definitions developed by Jonathan Shay in the 1990s and Brett Litz and a team of scholars more recently. As I review the term, I am also critiquing it. I split "moral injury" in two, treating "moral" in chapter 3 and "injury" in chapter 4. I am offering an additional working definition of moral injury as negative revelation: concisely, a "despair of the world and oneself." Chapter 3 deals with the "world," by which I mean normative claims regarding what is good, right, and just (summed in the word "moral"). Specifically, I address how just war theory becomes conflated with an assumption that wars actually waged are just.

I separate into two chapters, for the sake of clarity, that which cannot be separated in the life of a real person. Normative claims regarding what is good and just are located outside of the individual, while also deeply internalized by individuals. There are no collective/social normative claims about the good without individuals, and no individual can conceive of the good outside of her concrete social position. I also treat moral injury in two chapters because I do not wish to discard the fruits that moral injury discourse has offered by focusing on the individual. I am not arguing that moral injury literature that focuses on the trauma of individuals has been wrong; I am arguing that the literature is *incomplete* insofar as it brackets larger questions about social values and commitments, especially around war. The individual experiencing moral injury as negative revelation is not only coming to terms with the knowledge that she has betrayed her own values; she is coming to terms with the knowledge that the values of her own nation, in political and public rhetoric as well as concrete action taken in other nations, are already poisoned from within. There are choices for assigning blame and responsibility for what has gone wrong with this war, each true in part. I can blame myself; I can blame the Army; I can blame the Bush administration; I can blame "terrorists"; I can blame indifferent U.S. citizens. Each of these is worth a book length's treatment. In chapter 3, I am taking aim at a moral convention that treats "enemy" others as objects of hatred and domination.

Chapter 4 takes on the "injury" component of moral injury, by which I mean an individual's despair about the meaning of her life. I draw on Alasdair MacIntyre's notion of the narrative unity of a human life, as well as the creeds and oaths of U.S. military service, to offer a picture of the American soldier as an "intelligible self"—a self oriented toward a *telos* of war. I draw on the work of Susan Brison to show how the notion of an "intelligible self" and an ultimate *telos*, or purpose/meaning/end, of human life disintegrates. By the end of chapter 4, I am describing negative revelation and moral injury as an affirmation of meaninglessness—the "world's" claims on what is good, and one's own understanding of goodness, have been revealed as meaningless in the concrete reality of war. This affirmation is meaningful in that one finds oneself longing for genuine goodness and justice. As Paul Tillich puts it: "no actual negation can be without an implicit affirmation."[26] In my own words, by rejecting what is evil and unjust in war (rejecting anti-life), one is implicitly acknowledging the reality of goodness (affirming life)—despite not being able to feel its presence.

Chapter 5 is less about war and anti-life, and more an analysis in a phenomenological sense of "negative revelation." My primary interlocutors here are Emmanuel Lévinas, Friedrich Schleiermacher, and Dietrich Bonhoeffer. Respecting that their contexts are quite unique, I draw on these thinkers to show how a "revelation of the other" is life breaking through anti-life—the catalyst of negative revelation. It is my intention, by closing in this way, that life gets the last word, which is the truth regarding what I have learned through my own experience of negative revelation.

NOTES

1. George W. Bush, "Address to the Nation on the Terrorist Attacks," *Weekly Compilation of Presidential Documents* 37, no. 37 (September 17, 2001): 1301–302.
2. C.J. Chivers, *The Fighters: Americans in Combat in Afghanistan and Iraq* (New York: Simon and Schuster, 2018), xxii.
3. Origen, *On First Principles*, trans. G. W. Butterworth (Notre Dame, IN: Christian Classics, 2013), 129, 131.
4. Ibid., 125.
5. Michael Walzer's exposition of just war theory hinges on this moral equality: "the moral status of individual soldiers on both sides is very much the same: they are led to fight by their loyalty to their own states and by their lawful obedience. They

are most likely to believe that their wars are just, and while the basis of that belief is not necessarily rational inquiry but, more often, a kind of unquestioning acceptance of official propaganda, nevertheless they are not criminals; they face one another as moral equals." See Walzer, *Just and Unjust Wars: A Moral Argument with Historical Illustrations*, 5th edition (New York: Basic Books, 2015), 34–41, 127.

6. C.J. Chivers, *The Fighters*, xxii.

7. See, for example, Dietrich Bonhoeffer, *Ethics*, ed. Clifford J. Green, trans. Reinhard Krauss, Charles C. West, and Douglas W. Stott, *Dietrich Bonhoeffer Works*, Vol. 6 (Minneapolis, MN: Fortress Press, 2005), 366–370: "The ethical phenomenon is a boundary event, both in its content and as an experience. According to both its content and the experience, the 'ought' only belongs where something *is not*, either because it *cannot* be or because it is not *willed*."

8. Rita Nakashima Brock and Gabriella Lettini, *Soul Repair: Recovering from Moral Injury after War* (Boston, MA: Beacon Press, 2012), *xv*.

9. Paul Tillich, *The Courage to Be*, 3rd edition (New Haven, CT: Yale University Press, 2014), 5.

10. Simone Weil captures this absence and longing with the concept of "affliction," in which "there is nothing to love. . . . The soul has to go on loving in the emptiness, or at least to go on wanting to love, though it may only be with an infinitesimal part of itself." Simone Weil, "The Love of God and Affliction," in *Waiting for God* (New York: Harper Perennial, 2001), 67–82, 70.

11. Marcella Althaus-Reid, *Indecent Theology: Theological Perversions in Sex, Gender, and Politics* (New York: Routledge, 2000), 49.

12. Ibid., 49–50.

13. Ibid., 1–2, 71.

14. Ibid., 71.

15. H. Richard (Helmut Richard) Niebuhr, *The Meaning of Revelation* (Louisville, KY: Westminster John Knox Press, 2006), xxxiv.

16. Ibid., 4.

17. Ibid., 10.

18. Tim O'Brien, *The Things They Carried* (Boston, MA: Mariner Books, 2009), 171–72.

19. Ibid., 171.

20. Martha C. Nussbaum, "Finely Aware and Richly Responsible: Literature and the Moral Imagination," in *Love's Knowledge: Essays on Philosophy and Literature* (New York: Oxford University Press, 1990), 148–67, 162.

21. Ibid., 161.

22. Ibid., 161.

23. Althaus-Reid, *Indecent Theology*, 27.

24. Paul Tillich, *Dynamics of Faith* (New York: Harper and Row, 1957), 47.

25. Shelly Rambo, *Resurrecting Wounds: Living in the Afterlife of Trauma* (Waco, TX: Baylor University Press, 2017), 113.

26. Paul Tillich, *The Courage to Be*, 162.

Chapter 1

Anti-life

The Logic of War

... I have set before you life and death ...
—Deuteronomy 30:19 (NRSV)

The mystery of life contains within it a mystery of death. The death that belongs to life is a perishing, breathing one's last breath. It is the end of one integration of flesh and spirit, blood and dust, which will live again in some new and different way.

There is a logic of death that steals from the mystery of life. This is not the death that belongs to the mystery of life; it is anti-life, un-life, null-life. Anti-life resists change and perishing, and in doing so resists all life. The logic of anti-life wears the mask of life. It twists life into procedure, distorting the mystery of life and death into annihilation, desecration, and disintegration. Anti-life is affronted by the breath of life that grows, changes, and rests. Anti-life attempts to lock the breath of life in place, extinguishing life by explaining away its mystery.

Friedrich Schleiermacher puts the rhythm of the mystery of life simply, in the speech of the girl Sophie in his *Christmas Eve Celebration*. When asked whether she would rather be "merry or sad," Sophie says, "I always just like to be whatever I am at the moment."[1] Karoline, a woman at the party, later calls Sophie's attitude the "childlike sensibility ... without which one cannot enter into the reign of God. It is simply to accept each mood and feeling for itself and to desire only to have them pure and whole."[2] Sophie knows much about what it means to live; she expresses the mystery of life in its most basic terms, without attempting to explain it away. Sophie knows that joy comes with sorrow; the two are mingled together. She knows that life and death are mixed and interwoven. She knows it, and she cannot explain it. When pushed to explain her sensibility Sophie says to her mother, "he makes me uneasy with his questions, because I do not know how to arrange all that I am supposed to pull together to answer them."[3] Sophie accepts the mystery of life; she does not explain it.

Anti-life rejects what Sophie accepts. Anti-life rejects that life is open and changing, tending toward sorrow at least as often as it tends toward joy. In its rejection of life, anti-life brings about a sorrow beyond sorrow. Anti-life is an exhaustive explanation of life. Where life is filled with a multiplicity of purpose, anti-life reduces life to singular purposes. Where life is dynamic, anti-life is static, imprisoning life in rigid structures.[4] Where life branches out in innumerable directions, anti-life shears and cauterizes. Life is free and open-ended; anti-life is the prison of an imposed end.

Anti-life thrives in the hearts of people as a fear of death. Paul Tillich is right to distinguish fear from anxiety. Fear needs an object. Without an object to fear, there is only anxiety. Anxiety is always present as an awareness of finitude, the transitory and temporal nature of the mystery of life.[5] As young Sophie might well put it, anxiety is the awareness that our happiness might at any moment be disrupted by sadness, that death may appear at any moment to usher in the next stage of life while we are still busy living it in the ways in which we are accustomed. The anxiety produced by the condition of being finite—the very condition of the mystery of life—is not a thing. Anti-life cannot abide anxiety and so it makes death a thing, an object, and "objects are feared. A danger, a pain, an enemy may be feared, but fear can be conquered by action."[6] Anti-life persuades living beings to attempt to conquer death, but to conquer death is to conquer life itself.[7]

Anti-life is a rejection of and an assault on the conditions of life. Anti-life does not accept death. Anti-life makes death an object, gives it a face, makes it into a fearsome and terrible monster. Anti-life stokes the fear of death and promises immunity from death through the allure of a noble cause. It whispers the lie that if one dies in pursuit of the cause, then one has not really died, because the cause is immortal, eternal. This is anti-life's greatest sleight of hand. Disguised as a ward against death, it steals the mystery of death that belongs to life and twists it into death as necessity for a cause. Anti-life asks the insidious question, "Why die for nothing, when you can die for something?" The mystery of life becomes oriented toward an ideal end. However, the end offered by anti-life—whatever it may be in particularity—is never the end of life. Life cannot be exhaustively explained by a singular purpose. Death is an inevitable part of life (young Sophie knows this), but there is not any specific death that is a necessity. The logic of anti-life answers the fear of an unknown death with the certainty of a known death defined by the necessity of an urgent cause. People can conquer their fear of death by their willingness to die for the cause; through this exploitation of the fear of death, anti-life becomes the perpetual production of death. Anti-life's death is the feared monster, the object that anti-life beckons human beings to conquer through action. By reducing death to an object, anti-life also objectifies life. Life becomes fuel for the fight against death. The young are thus perpetually drawn into the endless old war. Anti-life shackles life with war.

I was a senior in high school when the World Trade Center was destroyed. I sat in a U.S. Economics class in rural Tennessee and watched, with my teacher and friends, as the usual DOW and Nasdaq numbers ticking along the bottom of the television screen gave way to something sinister. As a teenager in a small town, I was already anxious about my own finitude and restless to see the world. The attacks of 9/11/2001 hit me as an invitation to channel my anxiety and restlessness into action. Over the next several weeks, posters started appearing in the bedrooms of my friends—"most wanted" posters featuring Osama bin Laden and his suspected co-conspirators. As I enlisted in the Army the following spring, with my basic training deferred until I graduated high school, I remember feeling an electrifying sense of purpose. I had felt aimless in rural Tennessee, like my life did not much matter. My teenage angst had no outlet. Suddenly, my anxiety had been given a face—the face of Osama bin Laden—and the anxiety turned into a fear that could be conquered by action. It felt good to act. It felt good to put on a military uniform. It felt good to have purpose. I felt immortal and invulnerable. Such feelings are toxic. Osama bin Laden was not really the object of my fear. The "object" became anyone that looked or talked like him, and I did not really know much about him to begin with. However, at the time, it did not matter. I had purpose, and my purpose was to defend the United States against threats both foreign and domestic. I left it to my superiors (which, as an eighteen-year-old soldier, was essentially everyone in the Army all the way up the chain of command to the President) to decide who and what those threats were. I could say I was manipulated by those superiors, drawn into their war, which contains an element of truth. A more disturbing truth (and more complete) is the fact that I did not need much manipulation. I wanted an enemy, and I was given an enemy. I rejected the conditions of my own finitude; I welcomed the seduction of anti-life.

I write these words about myself, and they feel true. However, they leave something out: What about the possibility of a truly noble cause? Is there nothing to be said of the willingness to go to one's death for the sake of something beyond oneself? For example, "No one has greater love than this, to lay down one's life for one's friends" (John 15:13, NRSV). When I look back on my younger self with jaded eyes, I wonder what I could be forgetting. I was naïve to a fault, yes, but was I not courageous as well? Whether I was courageous or not—surely enlisting in the military is not the same thing as rejecting the conditions of finitude. Military service is not anti-life. What I am trying to say, as I move in circles around my memory and these tentative steps at a concept, is that military service is caught up in the same tensions between anxiety and fear in which all of existence is caught. Military service is not an escape from the tension and that, perhaps, is where my younger self erred. Anti-life is a perpetual assault on the structures of life, and this includes even the possibility of a truly noble cause—or in the absence of a truly noble cause, then a noble (if naïve) motivation.

Dietrich Bonhoeffer wrote, "Whenever Christ calls us, his call leads us into death"; or, in a more famous translation, "When Christ calls a man, he bids him come and die."[8] Is there nothing to be said for the willingness to answer this call? Surely this is not the same as anti-life's twist of death into necessity. The claim that will not let me go: there must be something worth dying for! And there is—life itself is worth dying for. It is the same paradoxical notion that only peace is worth a war—a paradox that so often tends toward war without ever any peace. Jesus's "call to death" is "the call which summons us away from our attachments to this world," or, as Bonhoeffer puts it earlier, the "costly grace" that "costs people their lives" and "thereby makes them live."[9] Self-denial, in this sense, is a denial of anti-life. The willingness to face death is an acceptance of the conditions of life; it is a liberation from the fear of death.

There is a fine line here that I wish to make clear. On the one hand, there is self-denial, a freedom from attachments to which one can be *too* attached. In other words, one can turn away from attachments to embrace life fully; this is what Bonhoeffer describes as Jesus's call to discipleship. On the other hand, there is a denial of self that is a rejection of the very conditions of life—this is attachment to a shadow of life in which death is a monster. Death is *not* a monster but a part of life itself; thus, attempting to conquer death due to fear of it belies a fear of life itself. All that I am trying to say here is that it is hard to discern the answer to the question: *What for?* For what/whom am I being called to die? For what am I willing to die? On the one hand, there is the greatest love—to lay down one's life for one's friends; on the other hand, anti-life: "If any question why we died, Tell them, because our fathers lied."[10]

I pause here to acknowledge that "anti-life" sounds rather cryptic as I begin to write about it. It may also be of concern to the reader that I begin with "anti-life" rather than life; this appears as a morbid choice for a first chapter. Before going any further, I wish to address these concerns of cryptic-ness and morbidity. First, on cryptic-ness: in my view, there are at least two ways writing may appear cryptic. The first way is that the writing is generally sloppy, loose, and unorganized. I do hope to avoid this. The second way in which writing appears cryptic is when the topic at hand is genuinely mysterious, when a writer is doing her best to describe something that evades description. In this sense, many of my favorite writers and thinkers are quite cryptic. I am using my own term "anti-life" because it forces me to focus on what I wish to bring to light rather than relying solely on concepts that have been developed elsewhere with precision and depth, though I will borrow from other thinkers' conceptual frameworks to uncover what I mean by "anti-life" and thus avoid, as much as possible, the sloppy version of cryptic-ness.

Second, on morbidity as a concern: I begin with "anti-life" because, unfortunately, it comes first in my own experiential order of discovery. When I went to war, I thought I had grasped a certain fullness of life—along with goodness and justice, as I wrote in the introduction. I was mistaken. Part of what it means to be mistaken about such foundational things has to do with the nature of anti-life and war's revelation.

The heart of this book is my claim that the experience of war brings with it a revelation; however, that which is revealed (e.g., goodness, justice, life) is revealed through encountering its negation. Simply put, one recognizes that which goodness and justice *are not*. The purpose of this chapter is to begin broadly so that I can dig as deeply as possible into the negation—what I am calling "anti-life." I use the terms "mystery" and "logic," applied respectively to life and anti-life, with a purpose I hope to make clear in the pages that follow. In this chapter, I attempt to *describe* the logic of anti-life with my own words and with the aid of concepts borrowed from other thinkers. At times I may use prescriptive and proscriptive language, and this is inherent to my use of life and anti-life as concepts: life is life as it should be; anti-life is life imprisoned, distorted—that which should not be. In the overall arc of the book, anti-life is recognized in war (though I do not claim that it is *only* operative in war). The recognition of this terrible negation of life stirs a longing for life as it should and could be. This chapter is a description of anti-life in two parts: what it is and what it does.

WHAT ANTI-LIFE "IS"

In this section, I am describing what anti-life, as the negation of life, "is." Describing what negation *is* prompts a variety of intellectual conundrums. I am less concerned with anti-life as an intellectual curiosity than I am concerned, as a living being, with how anti-life is encountered and experienced in moments of existential crisis and despair—most especially in and through events of war. Nevertheless, anti-life, as an assault on life, assaults the intellect as much as any other aspect of life. Describing anti-life is an attempt to wrap one's mind around that which is an assault on one's mind and life. Language has its limits here as it does anywhere. For help in dealing with the conundrum of what anti-life "is," I turn to Karl Barth (nothingness), Paul Tillich (non-being), and Hannah Arendt (ideology). These thinkers help me form my own description of anti-life: *a static, parasitic, explanatory assault on the inexhaustible mystery of life.*

The Assault of Nothingness

To flesh out my provisional description of anti-life, I turn first to Karl Barth to capture a language of "assault." *Anti-life is an assault on life.* Anti-life is akin to Karl Barth's concept of "nothingness," which has its own distinct quality of being real as "the antithesis which can be present and active within creation only as an absolute alien opposing and contradicting all its elements, whether positive or negative . . . offering only menace, corruption, and death, so that it must never be expressed in terms of synthesis."[11] Nothingness is "the comprehensive negation of the creature and its nature. . . . As negation nothingness has its own dynamic, the dynamic of damage and destruction with which the creature cannot cope."[12] In Christian terms (the terms with which Barth is primarily concerned), nothingness is that which "is alien and averse to grace, and therefore without it."[13] In short, according to Barth: God created the world, and this was an act of grace. The world is full of grace. In the act of creating, there is also all that which God did not create but rather "passed over and set aside, marking and excluding it as the eternal past, the eternal yesterday."[14] That which has been passed over is nothingness—it is all that is averse to grace. This is the sense I wish to capture with the logic of anti-life: it is all that is averse to life, and life is gracious (and mysterious).

Barth warns against misconceiving nothingness as part of the structure of life, as part of the death that belongs to life: "Light exists as well as shadow; there is a positive as well as a negative aspect of creation and creaturely occurrence."[15] These positive and negative aspects are the dialectic of "Yes" and "No" shot through creation as well as Barth's theology, which he occasionally summarizes poetically as in the following:

> It is true that in creation there is not only a Yes but also a No; not only a height but also an abyss; not only clarity but also obscurity; not only progress and continuation but also impediment and limitation; not only growth but also decay; not only opulence but also indigence; not only beauty but also ashes; not only beginning but also end; not only value but also worthlessness. It is true that in creaturely existence, and especially in the existence of man, there are hours, days and years both bright and dark, success and failure, laughter and tears, youth and age, gain and loss, birth and sooner or later its inevitable corollary, death. It is true that individual creatures and men experience these things in most unequal measure, their lots being assigned by a justice which is curious or very much concealed. Yet it is irrefutable that creation and creature are good even in the fact that all that is exists in this contrast and antithesis.[16]

In the passage above, Barth echoes the childlike sensibility of Schleiermacher's young Sophie. The "Yes" and "No" of life are two elements brought together in synthesis: living is also dying, and one dies only by living. Laughter and tears are mixed up together. Anti-life is not a part of this synthesis; like nothingness, as Barth calls it, anti-life is the antithesis to both living and dying, laughter and tears. Anti-life cannot bear the passionate joy and sweet sorrow of life, because joy and sorrow are reminders of impermanence. Anti-life is not light's shadow. Anti-life is not the "No" that complements the "Yes" of life; it is the anti-thesis to all synthesis, to life's "Yes" and "No."

In the Barthian landscape, nothingness is an assault on all of creation; nothingness is an "adversary"; nothingness "opposes and resists" God, and God likewise "opposes and resists nothingness"; nothingness "confronts" creatures as "final peril" and "threat and corruption."[17] Barth applauds Augustine for making privation "not just the absence of what is good but an *assault* upon it" (italics mine).[18] Barth captures something with nothingness that I am trying to capture with anti-life: *anti-life is an assault on life*.

The Stasis of Nonbeing

I turn to Paul Tillich for another glimpse of anti-life through the concept of "nonbeing." While Barth gives me the language of assault, Tillich provides a language of stasis. Building my provisional description of anti-life step by step, then, *anti-life is a static assault on life*. To be sure, the language of assault is not absent from Tillich. In Tillich's *The Courage to Be*, the assault is captured with "in-spite-of": "Courage is self-affirmation "in-spite-of," that is in spite of that which tends to prevent the self from affirming itself"; nonbeing is the 'in-spite-of.'[19] However, Tillich often does not give teeth to the "in-spite-of"; for example, James Cone must fill in the abstract "nonbeing" with the content of life to assert: "the courage to be black in-spite-of white racists."[20] In Cone's work, white racists are the concrete manifestation of Tillich's abstract "that which tends to prevent the self from affirming itself." Tillich's gift to theologians is in the abstract, the gift of a framework that Cone and others can use to pinpoint the existential horror of concrete situations—for example, racism and lynching.

Tillich helps me describe anti-life with the language of *stasis*, though stasis is more my way of describing the Tillichian concept I am getting at than Tillich's own language. Being is not static in Tillich's work. Tillich works with *dynamics*. Being is "life, process, becoming."[21] Nonbeing, on the other hand, is the negative that "lives from the positive it negates," and "being includes nonbeing but nonbeing does not prevail against it."[22] If being is life in process, becoming—that is, dynamic—then nonbeing is frozen life, motionless, static; it is the loss of dynamics to "rigid forms."[23] To paraphrase

Cone and Tillich—the courage to be black in-spite-of white racists is the courage to *live* and *breathe* and *move* and *become* in-spite-of a racism that *kills* and *suffocates* and *freezes* and *locks into place*.

Tillich is a theologian and philosopher of being. As a theologian, Tillich writes about "God." As a philosopher, Tillich writes about "Being-itself." As both theologian and philosopher, Tillich is writing about "God," not as a supreme being, but as "the initial power of everything that is," or "Being-itself."[24] The question of God, for Tillich, is the ontological question—"What is being itself?"—and it arises out of a "metaphysical shock—the possibility of nonbeing"; stated differently, "it is the finitude of being which drives us to the question of God."[25] The metaphysical shock of possible nonbeing, the awareness of human finitude, is an awareness of life's synthesis of "Yes" and "No" in Barth's work. Tillich also uses "nonbeing" to refer to the kind of absolute negation signified by Barth's nothingness, the absolute "No": "nonbeing is not a concept like others. It is the negation of every concept."[26] The dual meaning of nonbeing in Tillich's work is clarified by distinctions in the Greek language that English does not readily offer:

> The mystery of nonbeing demands a dialectical approach. The genius of the Greek language has provided a possibility of distinguishing the dialectical concept of nonbeing from the nondialectical by calling the first *me on* and the second *ouk on*. *Ouk on* is the "nothing" which has no relation at all to being; *me on* is the "nothing" which has a dialectical relation to being.[27]

Dialectical nonbeing (*me on*) is like Sophie's approach to being both merry and sad, or Barth's light and shadow: it is the tension between thesis and antithesis shot through the synthesis that is life itself. Nondialectical nonbeing (*ouk on*) closely resembles Barth's concept of nothingness—a third factor, an absolute negation of thesis, antithesis, and synthesis. Dialectical nonbeing has to do with the potentiality of being, whereas nondialectical nonbeing is the *nihil* of the Christian doctrine of *creation ex nihilo*—the nothing out "out of which God creates . . . the undialectical negation of being."[28]

Wrestling with the concept of nonbeing—dialectical or otherwise—on paper may appear painfully abstract, but I argue that these abstractions become critically important in the lives of human beings. Tillich puts it simply: "the dialectical problem of nonbeing is inescapable. It is the problem of finitude . . . being, limited by nonbeing, is finitude."[29] Life has limits—we become aware of our mortality and impermanence. We are "metaphysically shocked" as we recognize that though we are, we have not always been, and we will reach an end. For Tillich, accepting the anxiety produced by this awareness of finitude is *courage*. Life exists in the present, right here, due to an unknown cause, with a specific body; and yet, the present is fleeting, life does not remain in one spot, we cannot cause ourselves to be, and our bodies grow and decay. Courage is the acceptance of the anxiety produced by the dialectical tension of the mixture of being and nonbeing throughout every aspect of the mystery of life.[30]

As I flesh out this concept of anti-life as *a static assault on life*, the distinction between nondialectical and dialectical nonbeing is vitally important. I posit that both types of nonbeing can be seen clearly in the example of James Cone's application of courage already given above: "the courage to be in-spite-of white racists."[31] On the one hand, there is the generic awareness of life's finitude: life is threatened, it takes courage to affirm oneself, one's being, in the face of threat. On the other hand, racism is not part of the structure of life—I am making a proscriptive statement here. Death by lynching is different than growing old and passing away. The awareness of one's inevitable death demands courage and acceptance—and this courage and acceptance may indeed bolster one's capacity to be "in-spite-of white racists," but there is a third factor here, racism itself, that must not be accepted. Cone's "in-spite-of" does not give racism a pass; it is a rejection of racism and a commitment to live one's best life even in the face of the evil of racism. Therein is the decisive difference; death is not evil—it belongs to life. Death is nonbeing in dialectical tension with being. The production of death through racism is evil; it is a rejection of life. It is *ouk on*, nothingness, absolute negation. It is anti-life.

The "static" quality of anti-life is the link I am trying to get at between the dialectical and nondialectical ways of speaking of nonbeing, in Tillich's terms. In Barth's terms, I am establishing a link between the "No" that stands against the "Yes" and "No" of creation—the antithesis with which there can be no synthesis. Anti-life is not a synthesis, but it is a link between the concepts of dialectic tension and absolute negation. James Cone captures the link with "the courage to be in spite of white racists." The racism of white racists attempts to lock the dialectic movement of life into place. White racists do not have the courage to accept their own condition of finitude, and thus they try to freeze whiteness into a false superiority and blackness into a false inferiority. White racists attempt to give a permanent and infinite quality to white flesh—flesh that is as impermanent and finite as any other.[32] In Tillich's work, a move like this is demonic: "the claim of something finite to infinity or to divine greatness is the characteristic of the demonic."[33] Tillich goes on to say that "a main characteristic of the demonic is the state of being split . . . the elevation of one element of finitude to infinite power and meaning necessarily produces the reaction from other elements of finitude, which deny such a claim or make it for themselves."[34] Racism is an example of the demonic state of being split. Nationalism is another. There are a host of examples, and war as explored in this project will touch on many of them. What I wish to make clear here is the insidious nature of anti-life: what begins as an inability to accept the anxiety produced by the awareness of the conditions of finitude ends with accepting much worse—the absolute negation of those conditions. Or put another way: the fear of death and other negative poles of finitude becomes the rejection of life itself. Rejecting life's "No," or the dialectical tension of *me on*, is to orient oneself toward one's own absolute negation, toward *ouk on* and nothingness, toward anti-life. In the attempt to make permanent what is impermanent, anti-life assaults life with stasis and twists the fear of death into the production of death.

Before setting aside Barth and Tillich, I wish to make clear what I hope is already thoroughly implied: Anti-life is evil. I tend not to use the word "evil" very often because I have seen it too often applied to human beings—and the labeling of people as "evil" too often leads to a justification for killing them. Nonetheless, anti-life is evil; it is also not a person or being—though beings can unwittingly work toward the ends of anti-life. To borrow from Barth once more, anti-life is evil because like nothingness it is "averse to grace."[35] The way nothingness is evil is also a key to understanding its curious existence. Nothingness "is" only in relation to that to which it is averse—to grace. Grace is ontologically prior to that which is averse to grace. Nothingness is parasitic in this way, dependent on grace for its own shadowy existence. Nothingness is the Barthian version of the long-held theological affirmation that sin and evil have no substance. In Tillich's terms, nonbeing is dependent on being-itself:

> Being, limited by nonbeing, is finitude. Nonbeing appears as the "not yet" of being and as the "no more" of being. It confronts that which is with a definite end (*finis*). This is true of everything except being-itself—which is not a "thing." As the power of being, being-itself cannot have a beginning and an end. Otherwise it would have arisen out of nonbeing. But nonbeing is literally nothing except in relation to being. Being precedes nonbeing in ontological validity, as the word "nonbeing" itself indicates.[36]

I have already begun to fashion the next point in my provisional description of anti-life—that it is *parasitic*, though I flesh out the *parasitic* and *explanatory* nature of anti-life in what follows using the work of Hannah Arendt on "ideology." The final gift from Barth and Tillich in this section is the affirmation that life is ontologically prior to anti-life. Anti-life, as an assault *on life*, is parasitically dependent on life. There is no anti-life without life—though there can be life without anti-life. There will be more on this in the chapters to come, but Barth would put the observation this way: "nothingness has no perpetuity. God not only has perpetuity, but is . . . the basis, essence and sum of all being," and though God's creatures are finite, God wills to be in fellowship with them and thus even "finite and mutable" creatures have perpetuity through their connection to the divine.[37] To very loosely paraphrase Tillich, there is life "in-spite-of" anti-life—this "in-spite-of" is already an acceptance of the conditions of finitude and a rejection of and resistance to those forces which deny the conditions of life itself. Anti-life, unlike finitude, is not built-in to the structures of existence. Anti-life is not necessity—though it may appear pervasive. *Anti-life is a static assault on the mystery life*—a fear and rejection of the conditions of life that attempts to lock life decisively in place, murdering mystery with explanation.

The Parasitic Nature of Ideology

Anti-life is not merely an abstract concept. It can take hold of lives. Anti-life as *ideology* is the feature with which anti-life becomes concrete in the lives of people, just as nonbeing becomes concrete as white racism in the work of James Cone. Hannah Arendt's definition of ideologies: "-isms which to the satisfaction of their adherents can explain everything and every occurrence by deducing it from a single premise."[38] A totalitarian ideology, with which Arendt is primarily concerned, utilizes the single premise as a kind of "supersense" to logically justify totalitarian nonsense. For example, the "supersense" of Nazi mass murder: "if the inmates are vermin, it is logical that they should be killed by poison gas; if they are degenerate, they should not be allowed to contaminate the population; if they have "slave-like souls" (Himmler), no one should waste his time trying to re-educate them."[39] The words reek of nothingness, nonbeing, and nonsense. The pairs of statements, put into practice, become real and terrible despite their nonsensical nature. The "supersense" of ideological anti-life diminishes the mystery of life into nonsense:

> Once their claim to total validity is taken literally they become the nuclei of logical systems in which . . . everything follows comprehensibly and even compulsorily once the first premise is accepted. The insanity of such systems lies not only in their first premise but in the very logicality with which they are constructed . . . totalitarian regimes establish a functioning world of no-sense.[40]

Anti-life requires acceptance to take hold. Real people must accept a nonsensical first premise like "the inmates are vermin" in order to proceed "logically" to "they should be killed by poison gas." Anti-life, as ideology that has taken hold, fuses together the first premise and the "reality" put in place through the procession from the premise. That is, ideological "reality" comes to match the premise that spawned it: by killing inmates with poison gas, the Nazis diminished people to vermin. The "supersense" feeds back into the premise—only vermin are killed with poison gas; the inmates are killed by poison gas; hence, the inmates are vermin. When a totalitarian ideology has taken hold, the necessity of justifying such horrific actions disappears. The murderers no longer need to start with a premise to build their death camps; their death camps become the basis of the premise that warrants their existence.

I am not equating what I describe as "anti-life" with "totalitarianism" as Arendt defines it. Nevertheless, there are elements to Arendt's totalitarianism that are useful for clarifying the anti-life concept, namely, the way ideology functions. According to Arendt, "all ideologies contain totalitarian elements, but these are fully developed only by totalitarian movements, and this creates the deceptive impression that only racism and communism are totalitarian in character."[41] Anti-life is not dependent on totalitarian movements; it only needs certain ideological elements to take hold of the hearts of people in order to do its work. Nevertheless, to clarify my use of Arendt, I pause here to summarize her work on totalitarianism and ideology.

Totalitarianism, as both a movement toward and a holding of power, is "the permanent domination of each single individual in each and every sphere of life."[42] Going further with Arendt, the "total domination" at the heart of totalitarian movements "strives to organize the infinite plurality and differentiation of human beings as if all of humanity were just one individual."[43] Bringing these two together, then: totalitarianism treats humanity as one individual and dominates that individual in every sphere of life. Put in other words, totalitarianism is domination through diminishment, and diminishment is that aspect of Arendt's totalitarianism that anti-life shares. The assault of anti-life diminishes life to hold it in stasis. Ideology is the kind of thinking that sets the stage for the assault. Again, "all ideologies contain totalitarian elements," but "the real nature of all ideologies was revealed only in the role that the ideology plays in the apparatus of totalitarian domination."[44] Through her study of totalitarianism as movements and totalitarianism in power, Arendt outlines "three specifically totalitarian elements that are peculiar to all ideological thinking,"[45] and these three elements help to elucidate what anti-life is.

"First, in their claim to total explanation, ideologies have the tendency to explain not what is, but what becomes, what is born and passes away. They are in all cases concerned solely with the element of motion, that is, with history in the customary sense of the word."[46] Now, I have claimed that the mystery of life *is* about movement; with Tillich, "being" is "life, process, becoming."[47] For Arendt, ideologies are about the element of motion, but only in the sense that it attempts to move beings into an identity bestowed by the totality. The aim and "movement" of ideology is actually toward a stasis—a world in which there is only the fully accomplished realization of the ideology and the annihilation of everything else. "Ideologies are never interested in the miracle of being."[48] The movement of ideologies is not the movement of life or the miracle of being; ideological movement is only the "motion" of the "supersense," the "logical process" unfolding from the single first premise. Ideology's first premise, the slogan (i.e., propaganda), always involves a life—but it is life replaced by idea. This life is either inferior (by implication, other lives are superior); or, this life is superior (by implication, others are inferior). The movement of anti-life makes the first premise about life an unquestionable "law of nature" or "instrument of explanation"[49]—a principle behind all principles. Racism—the "idea" of racial superiority and inferiority—"moves" by the systematic destruction of lives based on race; ideology pretends that the movement is nature and history: "Racism is the belief that there is a motion inherent in the very idea of race." In this way, the mystery of life is reduced to an idea that "promises to explain all historical happenings, the total explanation of the past, the total knowledge of the present, and the reliable prediction of the future."[50] In this book, focusing on war, the instrument of total explanation through "movement" from first premise has to do with lives defined as "enemies." The mystery of life does not exclude the possibility of having an enemy. Anti-life, however, replaces the life of an enemy with an idea. Life = people. Anti-life = ideas about people, minus the people. Anti-life "moves" a plurality of lives toward annihilation by blanketly putting the idea of enemy in their place.

Arendt's second totalitarian element in all ideological thinking: "Secondly, in this capacity ideological thinking becomes independent of all experience from which it cannot learn anything new even if it is a question of something that has just come to pass."[51] In Arendt's study of totalitarianism in the twentieth century, this element has to do with secrecy and conspiracy—the way "ideological thinking becomes emancipated from the reality that we perceive with our five senses, and insists on a 'truer' reality concealed behind all perceptible things."[52] Arendt is largely concerned here with the political maneuverings/intrigue of the Nazis and Soviets, but this element is still applicable to anti-life as the logic of war. Experience in war can disrupt the "idea" of person as enemy; this is part of war's revelation. When the idea of a "terrorist/insurgent enemy" no longer matches the life of a person/people one encounters in war, then the mystery of life has disrupted the logic of anti-life, which replaces people with enemies. I will return to this disruption throughout the book.

Finally, Arendt's third element of ideological thinking: "Thirdly, since the ideologies have no power to transform reality, they achieve this emancipation of thought from experience through certain methods of demonstration."[53] I have already provided an account of this method of demonstration through Arendt's example of the horrific Nazi "demonstration" of the premise that people can be vermin by exterminating them as if they are vermin. According to Arendt, what was new in the terrible ideologies of the twentieth century was that "it was no longer primarily the 'idea' of the ideology . . . which appealed to [the totalitarian ideologists], but the logical process which could be developed from it."[54] Life is diminished by an idea, a first premise; then, both life and idea are devoured by the process:

> It is in the nature of ideological politics—and is not simply a betrayal committed for the sake of self-interest or lust for power—that the real content of the ideology (the working class of the Germanic peoples), which originally had brought about the "idea" (the struggle of classes as the law of history or the struggle of races as the law of nature), is devoured by the logic with which the "idea" is carried out.[55]

From this element of ideology, I borrow the concept of "devouring" to say that anti-life is *parasitic*, to complete a provisional description of anti-life: *Anti-life is a static, parasitic, explanatory assault on the inexhaustible mystery of life.* In chapter 2, I will move on from the first principle of the twentieth-century death camps. The twenty-first century has more than enough death to go around. I will argue that the parasitic premise of anti-life today is "America first" "American exceptionalism." The United States is a superpower that must demonstrate its superiority and its power. The idea of defense and security, dependent on a perpetual enemy, is devoured by the perpetual process and logic of preparing for and engaging in war. Before turning fully to the practices of the United States in the twenty-first century, I must attend to how anti-life achieves its work.

WHAT ANTI-LIFE "DOES"

What anti-life is becomes more horrific through what it does. Anti-life is a static, parasitic, explanatory assault on the inexhaustible mystery of life. What is worse than this? That anti-life masquerades as life. Anti-life "dupes" us.[56] I have drawn from Barth, Tillich, Arendt, and I will soon turn to Dietrich Bonhoeffer to flesh out a theoethical framework of anti-life. All these thinkers were responding in some way to the horrors of World War II and its aftermath. I need to make clear: I am not conflating any contemporary actor with Hitler or Stalin. I am suggesting, with this theoethical framework of anti-life, that there are certain parallels to be drawn between the responses of thinkers like Barth, Tillich, Arendt, and Bonhoeffer to the crises of their day, and our responses to the crises of our own. The last piece of the framework to put in place before moving to the concrete example of twenty-first-century U.S. war waging in chapter 2 is providing an account of what anti-life does in order to fulfill its assault on life: it masquerades as life itself. The commitments and agendas held by the architects of war are not necessarily the same commitments held by those who fight the wars. In order to get the young to toe the line set by the old and powerful, anti-life must masquerade as life—it must dupe the war fighters with morality.

I have already acknowledged a tension between a love that gives one the courage to lay one's life down for one's friends and the anxiety over death that seduces a person into acting out of fear. The masquerade of anti-life as life lies at the center of this tension. When Osama bin Laden became the object of my fear (and by extension, any person that could be conflated with or linked to him) against which I could act, anti-life was taking hold of my own love for life. The line between the love I felt for other U.S. citizens, especially those who were the victims of the 9/11/2001 attacks, and the hatred I felt for Osama bin Laden was thin and blurred. The hate depended on the love and devoured it—because the love carried within it the seeds of hatred. Love for others often comes with qualifications and distinctions.

Being human is a trait shared by all human beings. This core commonality is expressed in a multitude of languages; it is a basic sense of connectedness undergirding plurality and a sense of manifold uniqueness and diversity. Hannah Arendt calls it "the abstract nakedness of being human and nothing but human"; in political terms, before all formally codified human rights, it is the "right to have rights." However, Arendt warns and reminds that "the world found nothing sacred in the abstract nakedness of being human."[57] A quality of this abstract nakedness of being human is the mystery of life itself: the ever-present nearness of joy and sorrow, pleasure and pain, ecstasy and death. In the abstract nakedness of being human, we are living beings—fragile, flickering, and changing. Anti-life, the logic of war, proceeds from a parasitic premise that denies and assaults the mystery of life: there are humans, and there are beings that are seemingly human, which in fact are not human. These nonhumans are enemies—the object of attack. To be clear, by reducing some humans to subhuman, the humanity of all humans is diminished; those who are not categorized as subhuman are now implicitly superhuman—a denial of life as blatant as the diminishment to subhuman.

One could claim that in times of peace, human beings relate to one another in a way that holds sacred the nakedness of being human, while only in times of actual war and/or physical violence humans treat each other as less than human. I do not make that claim. I argue that actual war is merely a concrete demonstration of the logic of war, and this logic permeates social relationships as much in times of relative peace as it does in times of violent bloodshed. The event of our global war on terror exposes a singular moral framework, operating all along, that does not grant the status of being human to all human beings. Our global war on terror exposes that we have in fact been "duped by our morality,"[58] that we have been thinking, somewhere along the way, of humans as less than human.

Anti-life in the Form of Life

Dietrich Bonhoeffer provides a chilling account of how morality itself can become a tool of deception, a guise for anti-life. In his *Ethics*, which he never got to finish, Bonhoeffer describes the damage done not only to life, but also to morality, when anti-life masquerades as life: "That evil appears in the form of light, of beneficence, of faithfulness, of renewal, that it appears in the form of historical necessity, of social justice, is for the commonsense observer a clear confirmation of its profound evilness. Ethical theorists, on the other hand, are blinded by it."[59] Bonhoeffer described the era of Nazi Germany as a flash of lightning, in which "villains and saints" appeared again, "in full public view."[60] That flash of lightning blinded the masses from seeing the sacred in the naked human being. Bonhoeffer was trying to make the value of the human being visible again in Christianity, which had been thoroughly compromised in Nazi Germany. For Bonhoeffer, the value of the human being was at the heart of the doctrine of Incarnation, which he saw as the heart of Christianity itself. Bonhoeffer summarizes the doctrine concisely: "*Ecce homo*—behold God become human, the unfathomable mystery of the love of God for the world. God loves human beings. God loves the world. Not an ideal human being, but human beings as they are; not an ideal world, but the real world."[61]

Bonhoeffer saw his own time and place as "an era when contempt for humanity or idolization of humanity [was] the height of all wisdom."[62] Contempt and idolization are not love. Contempt and idolization comprise the split between subhuman and superhuman that serves as the foundation for the parasitic premise of anti-life. The capacity to see other human beings as subhuman is, perhaps, a capacity that all human beings hold—a bleak notion. However, I hope (I feel I must hope) that while contempt for human beings is a pervasive evil, the contempt is only explicitly and enthusiastically embraced for what it is by relatively few. Put another way, there are some who embrace anti-life, while there are many who are duped by it. In fact, it is precisely because many are duped by it that I am motivated to complete this book. Bonhoeffer said, "It is worse when a liar tells the truth than when a lover of truth lies, worse when a person who hates humanity practices neighborly love than when a loving person once falls victim to hatred."[63] Human beings often lie, and they often fall victim to hatred. This is different than claiming that human beings *are* all lying and hateful to their core. However, human beings can be manipulated and the capacity for hate can be shored up by hateful liars, and this is precisely what anti-life does as it masquerades as life. Bonhoeffer described this in his own context:

> At such a time the tyrannical despiser of humanity easily makes use of the meanness of the human heart by nourishing it and calling it other names. Anxiety is called responsibility; greed is called industriousness; lack of independence becomes solidarity; brutality becomes masterfulness. By this ingratiating treatment of human weaknesses, what is base and mean is generated and increased ever anew. The basest contempt for humanity carries on its sinister business under the most holy assertions of love for humanity.[64]

What Bonhoeffer describes is worse than a world that is not what it seems; he describes a world in which even the goodness of human beings is twisted to the point of non-recognition. Goodness is not merely obscured here but used to further cement a hatred for the other human being. Hatred itself masquerades under the guise of goodness.

In the world of moral inversion Bonhoeffer describes, he mourns six "rusty weapons" that "are not sufficient for the present struggle."[65] The first is reason; reasonable people will fail because they think they can "pull back together a structure that has come apart at the joints," but faced with the irrationality of the world they "withdraw in resignation or fall helplessly captive to the stronger party."[66] The second rusty weapon is a reliance on a purity of ethical principles; Bonhoeffer sees ethical theorists losing sight of a larger goal for the sake of arguing minutia. The third is a reliance on conscience, because one will always be tempted to settle for "an assuaged conscience rather than a good conscience."[67] Fourth is duty, because duty itself does not allow for the risk of a free action when it contradicts duty. However, those who rely on their freedom, the fifth rusty weapon, will fail because they are *too* willing to risk a bad action to prevent something worse. The final rusty weapon is a reliance on "private virtuousness," as those who rely on it "must close their eyes and ears to the injustice around them."[68]

Bonhoeffer is not disparaging the rusty weapons of ethics. The problem was that the world, in his eyes, had drastically changed. The best of intentions and motivations, founded on a love for life and human beings, are doomed to fail when the human being has already been assaulted, imprisoned, and devoured by a parasitic first premise. Hatred had already usurped goodness and justice. Anti-life pushes life away from its place at the foundation, replacing humanity with objects of idolization to be worshipped or objects of contempt to be feared. Bonhoeffer's tyrannical despiser can pay lip service to love, justice, and goodness, because those words are simply the masks of anti-life when reality has been conformed to divide life along lines of superiority and inferiority. In Tillich's words, humanity had "actually become what controlling knowledge considers [humanity] to be, a thing among things, a cog in the dominating machine of production and consumption. . . . Cognitive dehumanization has produced actual dehumanization."[69] Bonhoeffer and Tillich were both pointing to a sinister truth, which for them was manifested in a totalitarian social order: when certain assumptions or premises are accepted (knowingly or unknowingly), they take on a "life" of their own. Reasoned principles and pious virtues, if they are not aimed at the toxic premises themselves, only serve as more fuel for the fodder of anti-life.

Evil takes the form of light to do evil; anti-life takes the form of life to destroy life. The masquerade takes place at both the levels of reality and reflection on reality. That is, human beings are replaced by ideas about human beings—anti-life as ideology, and the destruction of life in reality reproduces ideals of destruction. Hannah Arendt captures this in her summary of the Nazis' "language rules": "it is rare to find documents in which such bald words as 'extermination,' 'liquidation,' or 'killing' occur. The prescribed code names for killing were 'final solution,' 'evacuation' . . . and 'special treatment.'"[70] Arendt goes on to say, "the very term 'language rule' was itself a code name; it meant what in ordinary language would be called a lie."[71] Echoing Bonhoeffer's horror at the liar who tells the truth, Arendt notes the "language system was not to keep these people ignorant of what they were doing, but to prevent them from equating it with their old, 'normal' knowledge of murder and lies."[72] A most striking example of a morally inverted world in which language and value have rotted from the inside out comes not from a Nazi, but from a doctor (who had never been a Nazi) called as a witness at Adolf Eichmann's trial in Jerusalem. At the trial, Dr. Servatius referred to "killings by gas" as a "medical matter," and stood by the claim when questioned by the judge: "it was indeed a medical matter, since it was prepared by physicians; *it was a matter of killing, and killing, too, is a medical matter.*"[73] When murder and medicine are synonymous, anti-life has succeeded at its masquerade.[74]

Bonhoeffer's observations regarding the failure of the "rusty weapons" of traditional ethics, though directed specifically at Hitler's Germany, can cut across time to offer a chilling warning to any society where "success is the measure and justification of all things. The world wants to be, and must be, overcome by success. Deeds, not ideas or intentions, are decisive. Success alone justifies injustice done. Guilt is scarred over, or cicatrized, by success."[75] Bonhoeffer's words are another way of framing Arendt's process of ideological devouring—the parasitic nature of anti-life. The 'motion' of a first premise takes over. In its nascent stages one must argue for the legitimacy of the premise, but soon enough reality and premise feed back into each other. What matters, in the end, is nothing but the "success" in which reality is a perfect mirror of the premise, and the premise is a perfect mirror of reality. This is an operation of anti-life; here, life itself has no value. Neither does justice or goodness. Guilt is scarred over in the flat, crystalline landscape of life purified of its imperfections—a landscape of total death.

Anti-life is the production of death through insidious means. In sum of what has been said so far: *Anti-life is a static, parasitic, explanatory assault on the inexhaustible mystery of life that masquerades as life itself.* I have borrowed concepts from thinkers who were wrestling with the horrors of World War II, both during and after the war. The era brought humanity and the world close to the brink of realized anti-life—a landscape of total death. In the next chapter, I will be using the framework of anti-life to make an argument about the foreign policy of the United States, specifically in and through the global war on terror. It is not a direct parallel to World War II, Nazi Germany, and/or the Stalinist USSR. However, the seeds of anti-life are present in the United States—especially in the premises of "America first" and "American exceptionalism."[76] Anti-life today is the logic of war, a devouring logic through which domination masquerades as freedom. Human beings are cognitively replaced and physically assaulted as adversaries, diminished to the role of adversary and held there in stasis, and their deaths are exhaustively explained by the premise of dominance masquerading as freedom and life.

NOTES

1. Friedrich Schleiermacher, *Christmas Eve Celebration: A Dialogue*, ed. and trans. Terrence N. Tice (Eugene, OR: Cascade Books, 2010), 37.
2. Ibid., 39.
3. Ibid.
4. See Paul Tillich, *Systematic Theology, Volume One* (Chicago: University of Chicago Press, 1951), 199: "Dynamics drives toward form, in which being is actual and has the power of resisting nonbeing. But at the same time dynamics is threatened because it may lose itself in rigid forms."
5. Paul Tillich, *Systematic Theology: Volume One* (Chicago: University of Chicago Press, 1951), 191.
6. Ibid., 191.
7. In the work of J. R. R. Tolkien, much suffering and bloodshed is rooted in the fear of death, a fear found especially in the hearts of powerful mortal rulers. "Men" [*sic*] are distinguished from elves in Tolkien's work by their mortality; elves live forever. The "men" resent death, but death was first given to them as a "Gift," a freedom from the world to which the elves were bound. However, the "Gift of Men" became known as the "Doom of Men," because the "thought of death darkened the hearts of the people." J.R.R. Tolkien, "Appendix A: Annals of the Kings and Rulers," in *The Lord of the Rings: 50th Anniversary One-Volume Edition* (Boston, MA: Houghton Mifflin Harcourt, 2005), 1033–1036. See also J.R.R. Tolkien and Christopher Tolkien (ed.), *The Silmarillion* (Boston, MA: Houghton Mifflin Harcourt, 2001), 41–42.

8. Dietrich Bonhoeffer, *Discipleship*, ed. Geffrey B. Kelly and John D. Godsey, trans. Barbara Green and Reinhard Krauss, Dietrich Bonhoeffer Works, Vol. 4 (Minneapolis, MN: Fortress Press, 2001), 87.

9. Ibid., 45, 87.

10. Rudyard Kipling, "Epitaphs: Common Form," in *The Penguin Book of First World War Poetry,* ed. George Walter (London: Penguin Books, 2006), 245.

11. Karl Barth, *Church Dogmatics III.3: The Doctrine of Creation*, ed. G.W. Bromiley and T.F. Torrance, trans. G.W. Bromiley and R.J. Ehrlich (New York: T&T Clark International, 2004). 302.

12. Barth, CD III.3, p. 310.

13. Ibid., 353.

14. Ibid.

15. Ibid., 295.

16. Ibid., 296–97.

17. Ibid., 290–310.

18. Ibid., 318.

19. Paul Tillich, *The Courage to Be*, 3rd Edition (New Haven, CT: Yale University Press, 2014), 31.

20. James Cone, *A Black Theology of Liberation*, Fortieth Anniversary Edition (Maryknoll, NY: Orbis Books, 2016), 57.

21. Tillich, *Courage to Be*, 31.

22. Ibid., 162, 165.

23. Tillich, *Systematic Theology, Volume One*, 199.

24. Ibid., 189.

25. Ibid., 163, 166.

26. Tillich, *The Courage to Be*, 32–33.

27. Ibid., 188.

28. Ibid.

29. Tillich, *Systematic Theology, Volume One*, 189.

30. This is a very brief paraphrase of "Finitude and the Categories" in Tillich, *Systematic Theology, Volume One*, 192–98. The four categories of time, space, causality, and substance are the "forms in which the mind grasps and shapes reality"—and these categories are "aspects of finitude in its positive and negative elements." This section of Tillich's *Systematics* closely parallels his *Courage to Be*.

31. Cone, *A Black Theology of Liberation*, 57.

32. For a chilling account of the value ascribed to whiteness in the United States, see Kelly Brown Douglas, *Stand Your Ground: Black Bodies and the Justice of God* (New York: Orbis Books, 2015).

33. Paul Tillich, *Systematic Theology, Volume Three* (Chicago: University of Chicago Press, 1963), 102.

34. Ibid., 103.

35. Barth, *Church Dogmatics* III.3, 353.

36. Tillich, *Systematic Theology, Volume One*, 189.

37. Barth, *Church Dogmatics* III.3, 360.

38. Hannah Arendt, *The Origins of Totalitarianism*, New Edition with Added Prefaces (New York: Harcourt, Inc., 1994), 468.
39. Ibid., 457.
40. Ibid., 457–458.
41. Ibid., 470.
42. Ibid., 326.
43. Ibid., 438.
44. Ibid., 470.
45. Ibid.
46. Ibid.
47. Tillich, *Courage to Be*, 31.
48. Arendt, *Origins of Totalitarianism*, 469.
49. Ibid.
50. Ibid., 470.
51. Ibid.
52. Ibid.
53. Ibid., 471.
54. Ibid., 472.
55. Ibid.
56. See Emmanuel Lévinas, *Totality and Infinity : An Essay on Exteriority*, trans. Alphonso Lingis (Pittsburgh, PA: Duquesne University Press, 1969), 21: "Everyone will readily agree that it is of the highest importance to know whether we are not duped by morality."
57. Arendt, *Origins of Totalitarianism*, 296–99.
58. Emmanuel Lévinas, *Totality and Infinity: An Essay on Exteriority*, trans. Alphonso Lingis (Pittsburgh, PA: Duquesne University Press, 1969), 21.
59. Dietrich Bonhoeffer, *Ethics*, ed. Clifford J. Green, trans. Reinhard Krauss, Charles C. West, and Douglas W. Stott, Dietrich Bonhoeffer Works, Vol. 6 (Minneapolis, MN: Fortress Press, 2005), 77.
60. Ibid., 76.
61. Ibid., 84.
62. Ibid., 85.
63. Bonhoeffer, *Ethics*, 77. I stop short of unleashing the term "evil" as Bonhoeffer did: "It is worse to be evil than to do evil." Again, I fear that seeing another as ontologically evil is a step often followed closely by killing them. Then again, I have the luxury of not living in Germany under Hitler's reign.
64. Ibid., 85–86.
65. Ibid., 78–81.
66. Ibid., 78.
67. Ibid., 79.
68. Ibid., 80.
69. Tillich, *Systematic Theology, Volume One*, 99.
70. Hannah Arendt, *Eichmann in Jerusalem: A Report on the Banality of Evil* (New York: Penguin Books, 2006), 85.
71. Ibid., 85.

72. Ibid., 86.

73. Ibid., 69.

74. Tim O'Brien presents another, more ambiguous account of anti-life's language games through his stories of U.S. soldiers in Vietnam: "They were afraid of dying but they were even more afraid to show it. They found jokes to tell. They used a hard vocabulary to contain the terrible softness. *Greased* they'd say. *Offed, lit up, zapped while zipping.* It wasn't cruelty, just stage presence. They were actors. When someone died, it wasn't quite dying, because in a curious way it seemed scripted, and because they had their lines mostly memorized, irony mixed with tragedy, and because they called it by other names, as if to encyst and destroy the reality of death itself." Tim O'Brien, *The Things They Carried* (Boston: Mariner Books, 2009), 19.

75. Bonhoeffer, *Ethics*, 88.

76. See Kelly Brown Douglas, *Stand Your Ground: Black Bodies and the Justice of God* (New York: Orbis Books, 2015). Douglas names "exceptionalism" as "America's original sin."

Chapter 2

Domination as Freedom
Anti-life and Global War

This chapter begins to apply the abstract concept of anti-life to the concrete reality of global war, focusing on the invasion and occupation of Iraq by the United States in the early twenty-first century. Anti-life is the production of death through insidious means: *a static, parasitic, explanatory assault on the inexhaustible mystery of life that masquerades as life itself.* Anti-life rejects the conditions of life, even while it masquerades as life. Anti-life today is the logic of global war, a devouring process unfolding from a first premise of domination masquerading as freedom or of war masquerading as peace as in George W. Bush's claim before his presidency: "The best way to keep the peace is to redefine war on our terms."[1]

This chapter will look at the invasion of Iraq as the outcome of anti-life logic, tracing how the logic of domination masqueraded as freedom before the war and how domination continues to produce death on a global scale. I use the speeches, memos, musings, and recollections of former U.S. secretary of defense Donald Rumsfeld to offer specific examples of anti-life logic. I am not arguing that Rumsfeld himself is the chief or only architect of the war or of anti-life; however, until he was replaced in 2006, he was the most visible and prolific spokesperson of the global war on terror. In my view, he is also a careful thinker. There is a vast record from which to draw regarding how Rumsfeld thought about the war on terror: copious amounts of paper memos he circulated throughout the Department of Defense, his memoir, and several years of his having to think out loud in front of the press attempting to articulate the rationality of an absurd war.

Recalling Hannah Arendt, "National Socialism" and "Bolshevism" were totalitarian movements of domination, rooted in an idea that had to be "constantly kept in motion: namely, the permanent domination of each single individual in each and every sphere of life."[2] What the United States has done and continues to do by waging its global war on terror is not totalitarian in that it does not attempt to dominate every individual in every sphere of life. Nonetheless, the movement of domination is the motivating force of the global war on terror; however, *permanent* domination in every sphere is not the goal. The goal of the U.S. global war on terror is more about *proving the capacity to dominate* and ensuring that every individual in the world knows that the United States has the power to dominate anywhere, at any time.

To pursue the capacity for domination, domination must masquerade as freedom and peace (a version of anti-life masquerading as life) in order to be an "American" manifestation of anti-life. Anti-life becomes a "morality," albeit a morality that dupes us. Donald Rumsfeld, reminiscing about the Cold War, claims: "we needed to ensure peace not only by being strong, but by being perceived as strong by those who would do harm to our country and our allies."[3] The United States sees itself as a strong force that liberates people from domination. It must be strong, so the story goes, to provide and protect freedom in the world. Politicians of all parties pay tribute to the authoritative rendition of the U.S. role in World War II and its subsequent role as the power responsible for spreading freedom to the rest of the world. For example, George W. Bush in a campaign speech at the Citadel in 1999:

> Our world, shaped by American courage, power and wisdom, now echoes with American ideals. We won a victory, not just for a nation, but for a vision. A vision of freedom and individual dignity—defended by democracy, nurtured by free markets, spread by information technology, carried to the world by free trade. The advance of freedom—from Asia to Latin America to East and Central Europe—is creating the conditions for peace.[4]

I do not challenge the notion that there is an American "vision" of "freedom and individual dignity." However, I do claim that a vision of domination lurks underneath and within the vision of freedom, producing a rotten fruit. That is, domination is a parasitic ideological premise within the vision of American freedom. Recalling Arendt, first premises in ideologies are a kind of "logical supersense," through which all events can be deduced and explained. The premises are then fused with reality, that is, the premises must be demonstrated through action. Then, reality feeds back into premise.[5] Anti-life as domination masquerades as the American vision of freedom. American "freedom" is demonstrated and fused with reality through the movement of domination in the global war on terror.

Arendt, writing of Hitler's "Final Solution," notes that correspondence referring to that program of murdering millions of people was "subject to rigid 'language rules'"; killing became "final solution," "evacuation," and "special treatment."[6] According to Arendt, "language rule" itself is a code word for lying and deceit, and "the net effect of this language system was not to keep these people ignorant of what they were doing, but to prevent them from equating it with their old, 'normal' knowledge of murder and lies."[7] I am convinced that the global war on terror operates with a similar system of language rules, but it is a system quite different than the "final solution." I give a sliver of the benefit of the doubt to leaders in the United States; unlike Hitler's program of mass murder, I do think that many of the architects of the Iraq war actually believed and still believe in the United States' capacity to "advance freedom" in the world. Whereas Hitler's regime developed a program of murder and devised code words to call murder by other names, the architects of the war on terror, in my view, uncritically accepted a set of code words such as "freedom" and ended up unleashing a program of murder. Put another way, the architects of the war on terror, and especially of the invasion and occupation of Iraq, thoroughly deceived themselves—either by refusing to see the poison pill of domination in their concept of freedom or by swallowing the pill whole and contributing to the masquerade.

WHAT WE KNOW: REFLECTING ON DONALD RUMSFELD

In order to show how anti-life becomes concrete, how domination masquerades as freedom in the global war on terror (especially in the invasion and occupation of Iraq), I begin by laying out a historical and conceptual framework of the war by focusing on human beings who contributed to its planning and execution. At the center of this historical and conceptual framework is Donald Rumsfeld, whose actions as secretary of defense from 2001 to 2006 are topics of significant controversy. At the helm of the Department of Defense during the attacks on the World Trade Center on September 11, 2001, Rumsfeld's planning, strategy, and thinking has had a profound influence on the department and the U.S. military's global posture that far outlasts his tenure in office. To be sure, Rumsfeld himself, or any other individual person, cannot be held solely accountable for all that transpired and continues to transpire as part of the United States' global war on terror. I am not interested in attacking Donald Rumsfeld the man or laying the blame for the invasion and occupation of Iraq at his feet. Nevertheless, his position as Secretary of Defense and his method to approaching tasks provide a unique picture of how human beings find themselves caught up in systems of anti-life, and how human beings both unintentionally and intentionally perpetuate it. To put it succinctly, the story unfolding in and around Donald Rumsfeld's tenure as Secretary of Defense is a story of anti-life taking hold, a story of the production of death in the name of life, a story of attempts to dominate life that lead to horrific consequences.

Rumsfeld is especially compelling in that he emphasizes "the importance of intellectual humility"[8]—the type of humility that is necessary for resisting the explanatory assault of anti-life that attempts to empty life of mystery. Rumsfeld famously described this intellectual humility and the limits of human knowledge in a 2002 press briefing:

> Reports that say something hasn't happened are always interesting to me because as we know, there are known knowns: there are things we know we know. We also know there are known unknowns: that is to say we know there are some things we do not know. But there are also unknown unknowns—the ones we don't know we don't know. And if one looks throughout the history of our country and other free countries, it is the latter category that tends to be the difficult ones. And so people who have the omniscience that they can say with high certainty that something has not happened or is not being tried . . . can do things that I can't do.[9]

Rumsfeld was known for sending copious paper memos called "snowflakes" as secretary of defense, in which he would meticulously question the underlying assumptions he heard in various briefings, meetings, preparations, and plans. Indeed, the second step of his four-step decision-making process is "identifying the major assumptions associated with the challenge at hand, always recognizing that they are based on imperfect information that can change or even turn out to have been incorrect."[10] Rumsfeld questioned many assumptions, but he did not question *all* assumptions. His philosophical exposition on unknown unknowns was given in response to a journalist questioning whether there was evidence of Iraq attempting or being willing to supply terrorists with weapons of mass destruction.[11] The United States invaded Iraq a little over a month after the press conference; Iraq's support of terrorists and stockpiling of WMD was already functioning as an unquestioned assumption that would become a death-dealing first premise by the time Rumsfeld reminded the public of the limits of human knowledge.

While Rumsfeld may have been committed to questioning assumptions associated with the challenge at hand, the challenge at hand was how to execute the invasion of Iraq, not discerning whether the United States was justified to do so. With the logical category of "unknown unknowns," Rumsfeld was demanding that anyone questioning assertions made by the Bush administration about Iraq, terrorists, and WMD to prove a negative. This intellectual skepticism is captured in another of Rumsfeld's favorite phrases: "the absence of evidence is not necessarily evidence of absence."[12] None of this relentless questioning of assumptions ever gets down to the assumption that

Iraq would and should be invaded. John McLaughlin, who served as (then CIA director) George Tenet's deputy, would later describe Rumsfeld's technique as creating a shift in the intelligence community:

> By faulting analysts for being too tied to the evidence—too tied to what they could confidently describe as facts—they had opened the door to the kind of leap of analysis that led the intelligence community to conclude, prior to the U.S. invasion of Iraq in 2003, that Saddam Hussein must have weapons of mass destruction.[13]

The Bush administration's hard sell of Iraq's nonexistent WMD program to the American public is well documented and well criticized. Even Rumsfeld admits to the failure in his memoir, though in a manner that obscures the "leaps of analysis" necessary to make the case to go to war in Iraq: "Powell [did not] lie about Saddam's suspected WMD stockpiles. The President did not lie. The Vice President did not lie. Tenet did not lie. Rice did not lie. I did not lie. The Congress did not lie. The far less dramatic truth is that we were wrong."[14]

My project is not aimed at proving Rumsfeld or others in the administration liars, nor am I focused on cataloging the numerous mistakes made by the administration during the global war on terror. The truth is, the United States began a prolonged global production of death in the war on terror, a production of death that masqueraded as life to the American public. This was anti-life made concrete on the world stage. I begin this analysis of concrete anti-life with Donald Rumsfeld because I am committed to a task to which he himself is rigorously committed: questioning assumptions. The assumption of WMD stockpiles in Iraq was false, but that assumption is the low-hanging fruit. I am interested in the assumption(s) *behind* the assumption of WMD. What are the kinds of assumptions that lead to "leaps of analysis"—a sort of inevitable and inflexible certainty in planning for war based on the *absence* of evidence?

The category of "unknown unknowns"—that which one does not know that one does not know—is the key to Donald Rumsfeld's own assumptions regarding the role of the United States as a global power. Unknown unknowns catch people by surprise. Rumsfeld believes that being caught by surprise can be mitigated through the use of imagination: "I saw preparing for the inevitability of surprise as a key element in the development of defense strategy. We had to consider our vulnerabilities with imagination."[15] For Rumsfeld, the Pearl Harbor attack in 1941—as well as the World Trade Center attack in 2001—demonstrated a failure of imagination in the intelligence and defense communities. Reflecting on his confirmation hearing for his second stint as secretary of defense, Rumsfeld recalls being worried about the quality of U.S. intelligence:

We needed an ability to uncover what our enemies were thinking and what motivated them. I believed that with more knowledge of that sort we would be better able to alter an enemy's behavior before they launched an attack, rather than waiting and having to take action after an attack.[16]

The sort of knowledge Rumsfeld believes the United States needs is knowledge of the "unknown unknown"—the type of knowledge that would destroy the category with which Rumsfeld is so fascinated. Rumsfeld knows that he will be surprised. Rumsfeld attempts to prepare for surprise by imagining every possible surprise, knowing that the surprise is inevitable. The surprise will be something unimagined. A primary unquestioned assumption in Rumsfeld's approach to surprise—or the "unknown unknown"—is that surprise always equals threat. The inevitable surprise is some unforeseen danger, an unanticipated attack, an unwanted outcome. One can understand this view, especially when held by a secretary of defense on the job in September 2001. However, surprise—the unknown unknown—is also life itself, the inexhaustible mystery of life.

In the 2014 documentary *The Unknown Known*, historian Errol Morris interviews Donald Rumsfeld at length. Morris asks Rumsfeld, "How do you know when you're going too far?" Rumsfeld replies:

You can't know with certainty. All the easy decisions are made down below. When you say, "How can you know?" the answer is you can't. Wouldn't it be wonderful if we could see around corners? . . . have our imaginations anticipate every conceivable thing that could happen and then from that full array and spectrum, pick out the ones that will happen.[17]

Rumsfeld is a paradoxical thinker. It is evident that he is enthralled by the limits of human knowledge. He delights in describing the limits. It is also evident that he desires to overcome those limits, even while remaining convinced that they cannot be overcome. Rumsfeld speculates that it would be wonderful, essentially, to be both omniscient and omnipotent—that is, to be able to foresee all possible outcomes along with the ability to make one's desired outcome come to pass. This is how anti-life takes hold of people and becomes concrete: domination masquerades as the freedom to choose, though it is the rejection of life's conditions of uncertainty and vulnerability. When faced with the inevitably of surprise and the incapacity to make desired results come to pass, the possibility of complete control prompts a former secretary of defense to speculate: "Wouldn't it be wonderful?"

Toward the end of Morris's documentary on Rumsfeld, he has Rumsfeld read one of his old memos about knowns and unknowns from a screen, and Rumsfeld reflects on what he meant:

[Donald Rumsfeld, reading aloud]:
February 4, 2004
Subject: What you know.
There are known knowns. There are known unknowns. There are unknown unknowns. But there are also unknown knowns. That is to say, things that you think you know that it turns out you did not.
[Rumsfeld reflecting on what he just read aloud]: If you take those words and try to connect them in each way that is possible, there was at least one more combination that wasn't there, the unknown knowns. Things that you possibly may know that you don't know you know.
[Errol Morris:] But the memo doesn't say that. It says that we know less, not more than we think we do.
[Rumsfeld:] Is that right? I reversed it? Put it up again. Let me see.
[Rumsfeld reading again, slowly]: There are also unknown knowns. That is to say things that you think you know that it turns out you did not.
[Rumsfeld:] Yeah, I think that memo is backwards. I think it is closer to what I said here, than that. Unknown knowns. I think you are probably, Errol, chasing the wrong rabbit here.[18]

Rumsfeld gets at two truths in these descriptions of the "unknown known," the fourth and final category of his epistemological musings aimed at the "what" of human knowing. In his own fifteen-year-old memo that he is reciting aloud, Rumsfeld is describing a realm of error or miscalculation—*mistake*. Rumsfeld's reflection on the memo describes something different—the more accurate rendition of "unknown known," in a purely logical sense. That is, following the other logical/grammatical combinations of the two words "known" and "unknown," the "unknown known" would be that which one does not know one knows. That which one thinks one knows and in fact does not (what the memo describes) is *mistake*.

Both the logical "unknown known" and the realm of mistake are important aspects of war and revelation. I thought I knew freedom, but I did not. I came to know that "freedom" as I knew it was domination. I came to know that I was *mistaken*. I know that which others do not know they know (and that which they refuse to remember)—that America has a vision, not of freedom, but of domination.

Rumsfeld knew that involvement in the "middle east" would bring disaster, that it would be much harder to get out than to get in. Rumsfeld also knew, as a young congressman, the mistakes of the Vietnam War.[19] By 2001, Rumsfeld no longer knew what he knew. It is as if he were taken by surprise, finding himself in the driver's seat of a war gone off the rails. The category of what one thinks one knows, but it turns out one did not, covers a multitude of death in the global war on terror unleashed by the Bush administration. The category of rejection and denial of knowledge obtained, the logical form of "unknown known," covers the rest.[20]

KNOWING DOMINATION

Rumsfeld's epistemological musings are aimed at describing the "what" of knowledge. What do we know? What is the object of our intellect? There is a deeper and more ancient epistemological question that focuses on "how" we know at all. Here, the intellectual capacity to dissect the "what" of human knowledge always comes second to the immediate "how"—the experience of knowing (and not knowing). First, there is the *feeling* of knowing. Consciousness. How do I know the known? I feel the presence of domination; thus, I know it. I feel the absence of goodness and justice; thus, I know them. It is easy, from a distance, to be mistaken in thinking that the American vision of freedom is actually freedom. When confronted with a disquieting suspicion that domination lurks within that vision, one can choose to reject that knowledge. However, when one *feels* domination masquerade as freedom and is involved oneself in that masquerade, the veil is torn away. More will be said regarding this negative revelation in chapter 3; the remainder of this chapter will continue to focus on the *logic* of anti-life that precedes the embodied reality of war.

Anti-life as domination, masquerading under the American "vision" of freedom, takes several forms as it laid the foundation for and became concrete in the U.S. global war on terror. In the following pages I provide three examples: domination through military power, domination through political power (to redefine rules and people), and domination through a pretense of moral superiority.

Full Spectrum Dominance—Domination through Military Power

The strategic term "full spectrum dominance" is not a creation of the Bush administration, though it is often linked by critics to the overreach of the administration's global war on terror. However, the assumption that leads to a strategy of full spectrum dominance echoes throughout history in the notion that peace is something that must always be enforced with power and strength. Rumsfeld himself, throughout his career, rarely missed an opportunity to remind those around him that "weakness is provocative. Time and again weakness has invited adventures which strength might well have deterred."[21] Here an American "vision" of peace carries with it the assumption that the peace envisioned requires domination—or at least the knowledge that domination is always a present possibility.

"Full spectrum dominance" was thoroughly defined and adopted in the year 2000 by the Joint Chiefs of Staff, as the strategic goal the U.S. military would work to achieve by the year 2020. An exposition of "full spectrum dominance" was made available for unlimited public use with the summer 2000 release of "Joint Vision 2020: America's Military—Preparing for Tomorrow."[22] The focus of the document, "the need to prepare now for an uncertain future,"[23] echoes Donald Rumsfeld's own discomfort with the inevitability of surprise. The way the U.S. military can prepare for an uncertain future, essentially, is aiming for the capacity of world domination. I argue that dominating the world is not a hyperbolic interpretation of full spectrum dominance or "Joint Vision 2020." Dominating the world is, rather, a concise summary of goals outlined in the report.

"Full spectrum dominance" is defined as "the ability of U.S. forces, operating unilaterally or in combination with multinational and interagency partners, to defeat any adversary and control any situation across the full range of military operations."[24] The ability to defeat anyone and control anyone and anything is the goal. It is easy to get lost in the military language of the report describing the various capacities and operations that must be in place and mastered in order to achieve full spectrum dominance (e.g., information superiority, technological innovations, dominant maneuver, precision engagement, full-dimensional protection, and focused logistics). Nevertheless, full spectrum dominance is the capacity for world domination. This is a distinctly American, twenty-first-century version of world domination—one not rooted in the attempt to exert control over the everyday affairs of governments across the globe. This version of world domination is about ensuring, through the demonstration of the United States' capacity and will to dominate any given situation with military power, that the world will function in ways that align with American interests.

Domination is explicit in the term full spectrum *dominance*; the world that the United States needs to be able to dominate is represented in the phrase *full spectrum*. The "range of military operations" (full spectrum) across which any situation must be controlled spans from "combat" to "noncombat"; in military operational terms, "combat" is "war" while "noncombat" is "military operations other than war." There are three "general U.S. goals" across that range: in war, the goal is to "fight and win"; between war and other operations, the goal is to "deter war and resolve combat"; and, at the noncombat end of the range, the goal is to "promote peace and support U.S. authorities."[25] Thus, the full range of military operations—that across which the military must be able to control any situation—includes war, peace, and everything in between.[26] Furthermore, "given the global nature of our interests and obligations, the United States must maintain its overseas presence forces and the ability to rapidly project power worldwide in order to achieve full spectrum dominance."[27] It is not hyperbole to equate world domination with full spectrum dominance; it is simply a summary of the concept. Faced with an uncertain future, "full spectrum dominance" assumes all uncertainty and surprise is threat and meets the threat with an attempt to foresee and control all possible outcomes. "Full spectrum dominance" is the premise of domination put into the language of military strategy.

"Full spectrum dominance" is a message to the world that the United States has the capacity and the will to respond with destructive force should its interests be threatened. Chris Hedges puts it poignantly as he reflects on his time spent with young militants in Cairo following the Persian Gulf War: "The message that was sent to them was this: We have everything and if you try to take it away from us we will kill you."[28] John Tirman analyzes Desert Storm through Operation Iraqi Freedom as one long, continuous war that has little to do with governments and everything to do with markets:

> That this region has been resistant to U.S.-led economic globalization braces the mind-set of U.S. policy elites. But it is the singular significance of oil that forms the backdrop, the incentives, the foundation, and the near-hysteria associated with the region (e.g., animus toward Iranians, slavishness to Saudis), and the primary factor explaining the unshakable obsession with Iraq. Whatever one makes of the outcome of this long war, the costs and its rewards, it has been done for oil.[29]

Behind Rumsfeld's assumption that "weakness is provocative" is the premise that the United States is entitled to take what it wants from the world. Full spectrum dominance is the brute force through which the United States tries to stop other nations from responding in kind.

"American Sovereignty"—Domination through Political Power

"Full spectrum dominance," domination through military power, provides the raw material and means for the U.S. invasion of Iraq in 2003 while still waging war in Afghanistan. The raw capacity to dominate does not, however, provide a rational justification for doing so. Demonstrating the capacity to dominate the world depends on politics in order to put the machinery of full spectrum dominance into motion. The type of political justification that sustains global war is the concept of "sovereignty," but a unique kind of sovereignty that demands some exposition. I argue that a specific understanding of American sovereignty, the understanding that puts the global war on terror in motion and sustains it over time, is one more disguise through which the parasitic premise of domination can masquerade as freedom and wreak havoc. Donald Rumsfeld's understanding of sovereignty, in his own words, does not seem like such a parasitic first premise at face value:

> I think of sovereignty in concrete terms. It is a matter of freedom and autonomy. It means that we Americans control our destiny and are not ruled from abroad by officials we did not elect and courts we cannot hold accountable. Sovereignty is integrally tied to democracy, the right of Americans to choose their own leaders, to make their own laws, to limit the powers of government, and to enjoy due process of law.[30]

Context matters. Rumsfeld's view on American sovereignty is in the chapter of his memoir dealing with his own campaign to secure Article 98 agreements from other nations, ensuring that they would never surrender Americans into International Criminal Court custody after Rumsfeld himself is named in a lawsuit regarding a Yemeni detainee at Guantanamo.[31] The even broader context is that Iraq itself regained sovereignty on June 28, 2004. Rumsfeld recalls that he was at a NATO summit meeting in Istanbul on that day, thinking about Iraq as he met with allies: "I wondered if decades from now Americans might look back on the liberation of those long repressed Iraqis with the same kind of satisfaction that we felt about our liberation of Europe from Nazism and Soviet communism."[32] Sitting with the U.S. delegation, Condoleezza Rice was handed a cable noting that Paul Bremer had dissolved the Coalition Provisional Authority (the temporary government put in place after the invasion) in Iraq. Rice handed Rumsfeld the cable after writing "Mr. President, Iraq is sovereign." Rumsfeld handed it to President Bush, who in turn wrote "Let Freedom Reign!"[33] Theoretically, in June 2004, Iraq regained sovereignty; according to Rumsfeld's own definition, that should mean freedom and autonomy, a control of their own destiny, and not being ruled from abroad. The rest of 2004 saw increased levels of violence in Iraq, and the United States officially launched a counterinsurgency campaign under General Casey.[34] The occupation of Iraq was just getting started.

It seems likely that Rumsfeld would view military occupation from a foreign power as an encroachment on American sovereignty; however, Iraq's sovereignty was celebrated by the Bush administration while the U.S. military continued to wage a violent counterinsurgency campaign through the neighborhoods of Iraq. Iraq's first post-war minister of defense, Ali A. Allawi, reflects on this period: "The politics of reducing the definition of progress to a set of rigidly observed milestones had already set in. . . . Image frequently overwhelmed substance as the USA set one symbolic goal after another in the political process."[35]

What was unfolding, underneath the celebration of "freedom" and "sovereignty," was the premise and demonstration of domination. Daily, U.S.

convoys would go on patrol, moving from one point to another on predictably dangerous routes. The U.S. military and Iraqis thought to be aiding the U.S. military were targets of improvised explosive devices, vehicle borne improvised explosive devices, and suicide bombers. Nightly, U.S. forces would conduct "cordon and sweep" operations, detaining thousands of Iraqis over the course of the "counterinsurgency" versus "insurgency" campaign, often "unable to figure out who was of value and who was not."[36] The tactic for reducing the daily attacks on convoys was detaining and questioning Iraqis. "Sometimes units acted on tips, but sometimes they just detained all able-bodied males of combat age in areas known to be anti-American," often by kicking down doors and interrogating men in front of their families in the middle of the night or hastily removing them from their homes.[37] This, predictably, led to greater animosity toward U.S. forces and more daily attacks. Safety and security were much needed after the invasion, what was delivered was a static pattern of domination and terror as infrastructure continued to fall into disrepair.[38] Dexter Filkins describes the pattern: the "insurgency . . . was everywhere and nowhere. The Iraqis had to survive . . . life among the Americans often meant living a double life, the one they thought the Americans wanted to see, and the real one they lived when the Americans went home."[39]

The truth is chillingly simple: American sovereignty tends to mean something different than any other nation's sovereignty. George W. Bush had claimed on the campaign trail, "the best way to keep the peace is to redefine war on our terms";[40] the redefinition of war is inextricably tied to the ongoing redefinition of sovereignty, part of a logic of anti-life that started before the invasion of Iraq and gained momentum during the war. "Sovereignty" in the global war on terror redefines war, and it redefines human beings.

Firstly, "sovereignty" is amended to redefine war itself, breeding the doctrine of preemptive war. In his June 1, 2002, graduation speech at West Point, President Bush outlined the need for preemptive war by claiming that "in defending the peace, we face a threat with no precedent."[41] In order to confront the unprecedented threat, a method of warfare beyond "the Cold War doctrines of deterrence and containment" was needed, because "if we wait for threats to fully materialize, we will have waited too long." Self-defense, the right of any sovereign nation, becomes offense (aggression) in Bush's redefinition of war: "We must take the battle to the enemy, disrupt his plans, and confront the worst threats before they emerge." Invoking the machinery of full spectrum dominance, Bush warned that the "military must be ready to strike at a moment's notice in any dark corner of the world. And, our security will require all Americans . . . to be ready for preemptive action when necessary to defend our liberty and to defend our lives."[42] In other words, sovereignty and the protection of life are redefined to include the domination of other lives by disregarding the sovereignty of other nations.

A memo from Rumsfeld on August 24, 2002, attempts to justify Bush's redefinition of war to include preemptive action by making exceptions to the general rule of sovereignty: "the most compelling reason *for making an exception to the traditional concept of sovereignty is the danger posed by weapons of mass destruction*" (italics original).[43] Beyond WMD, Rumsfeld lists several other circumstances, which "lead inevitably to a doctrine of anticipatory self-defense." Anticipatory self-defense is another word for preemptive war, which is another word for the overriding of another nation's sovereignty. The language rule working here allows one to support the exception to sovereignty by associating preemptive war with "defense" rather than blatant aggression. Acknowledging that making exception to the general rule of sovereignty is "unsettling," Rumsfeld poses several questions at the end of his memo under the heading "Consider the alternatives," including:

> If the U.S. were severely constrained in the world, wouldn't that mean that regional powers would be freer to attack their neighbors, as Iraq invaded Kuwait? If the threat of U.S. action against states that develop and use WMD were to disappear, would the rights of others be safer? Would there be less or more incentive for additional countries to acquire WMD? Wouldn't peaceful countries be faced with a greater threat from hostile neighbors?[44]

Here Rumsfeld is attempting to challenge assumptions—but *not* the assumption that the United States should be able to engage threats "preemptively." He is placing the burden on those *against* the doctrine of preemption—challenging their assumption that preemption and "anticipatory self-defense" is a misguided and dangerous doctrine (aggression by other names). He writes as if preemptive action were the long-standing doctrine, that without it "the threat of U.S. action . . . would disappear," when in fact the threat of U.S. action is present *without* a doctrine of preemptive action or anticipatory self-defense. Preemptive action becomes codified in *The National Security Strategy of the United States of America*, issued by the Bush administration in 2002, thereby accomplishing Bush's goal of redefining war and allowing the anti-life premise of domination to unfold under the disguise of sovereignty and defense.[45]

Secondly, sovereignty as political domination redefines human beings, so that the machinery of full spectrum dominance can be unleashed upon them, anytime and anywhere. In the context of the global war on terror, detainees suspected of terrorism were eventually redefined as "unlawful enemy combatants," thus not receiving the rights accorded to prisoners of war under the Geneva Conventions.[46] Put another way, the anti-life version of sovereignty entailed capturing people within other sovereign nations and treating them as stateless. According to Rumsfeld, "terrorists were enemies, not criminals," thus they were given trials by military commissions rather than civilian courts or UCMJ tribunals: "The fact that the detainees were different was exactly the reason military commissions were different."[47] Anti-life falsely divides real human beings into unreal superhumans and subhumans. "American sovereignty" as the political guise of domination in the global war on terror puts this dehumanization into motion by relegating other nations' sovereignty to lesser status.

While detainees are stripped of their rights under the Geneva Conventions in order to be tried by military commission because they are suspected of breaking the laws of war, Rumsfeld elevates the rights of "Americans" by calling international courts "encroachments on our sovereignty." Rumsfeld believes the "greatest casualty" of that encroachment "will be the loss of America's willingness to use our military as a force for good around the world."[48] In other words, "American sovereignty" redefines war and human life in order to justify the United States' capacity to dominate, as well as the demonstration of that capacity.

The division of human beings into superhuman and subhuman becomes concrete in the everyday occupation of Iraq in several ways. As previously mentioned, the cordon and sweep operations were more about exacting vengeance for harm done to U.S. military personnel and allies. This was "the logical outcome of making force protection a top priority in U.S. military operations," but as Thomas Ricks rightly notes, "if keeping soldiers alive is the top goal, that could be achieved simply by staying at home."[49] Moreover, the world viewed the degradation of justice in the abuse of detainees at Abu Ghraib in 2004. I argue that one cannot undermine the human rights of prisoners with official policy and simultaneously be shocked that prisoners are abused.

The clearest demonstration of concrete anti-life in the war on terror is the most widely "known unknown." At any point, one can find the precise number of U.S. war casualties, both military and civilian, both deaths and injuries.[50] Despite many efforts, the number of Iraqi casualties remains a known unknown; the anti-life element of this knowledge gap was expressed by Rumsfeld himself: "Well, we don't do body counts on other people."[51] What *is* known is a vast disparity in the number of U.S. and Iraqi casualties. Since the global war on terror was launched, as of the time of this writing (August 3, 2021), 6,858 U.S. military personnel and civilians have died, with 52,441 wounded in action. The most conservative efforts to count Iraqi *civilian deaths* since the war began are in the hundreds of thousands, while moderate estimates put it over a million. This is to say nothing of the millions displaced by the war.[52] As a U.S. Army veteran, I usually recoil at the reduction of human beings to numbers. Those numbers have stories and lives. However, the Iraqis have been even further reduced by anti-life in war; their lives are not even marked by a number but by a range of estimates. Chris Chivers poignantly names anti-life's concrete ranking of some human life as more valuable than other human life, speaking here only of those who joined security forces aiding the American project in the war on terror: "well-intentioned Afghans and Iraqis gambled on American promises, only to suffer and die in quantities far exceeding the American loss of life. Blame for their shortfalls cannot fairly be assigned only to them. They were victims of Pentagon folly, too."[53]

Good and Evil—Domination through a Pretense of Moral Superiority

The third and final disguise domination wears in order to masquerade as the American vision of freedom in the global war on terror is the most basic, and the disguise on which anti-life in the United States most fundamentally depends. Military domination (full spectrum dominance) and political domination (sovereignty) could never be sustained without the assumption that the United States is in a position of global moral superiority. President George W. Bush, again in his 2002 graduation speech at West Point, articulated the assumption of moral superiority clearly:

> Some worry that it is somehow undiplomatic or impolite to speak the language of right and wrong. I disagree. Different circumstances require different methods, but not different moralities. Moral truth is the same in every culture, in every time, and in every place. Targeting innocent civilians for murder is always and everywhere wrong. Brutality against women is always and everywhere wrong. There can be no neutrality between justice and cruelty, between the innocent and the guilty. We are in a conflict between good and evil, and America will call evil by its name. By confronting evil and lawless regimes, we do not create a problem, we reveal a problem. And we will lead the world in opposing it.[54]

Bush does not speak the same language as Rumsfeld. There is no awareness of "unknowns" or any pretense of intellectual humility in the rhetoric that claims absolute moral truth and claims it once and for all for America. The world is torn in two. America is not only on the "good" side of a conflict against "evil"; America has the power and capacity to *name* what is evil for the rest of the world, to "call evil by its name." A crucial part of this vision of moral superiority that puts the premise of domination into *motion* is the assumption that the world must be *led*. Who better to lead the world than the nation with the military and political capacity to dominate any situation, anywhere in the world? Who better than the nation with "a vision of freedom and dignity"? Who better than the "good" nation with the power to name "evil"? Donald Rumsfeld himself asked a similar question, with some urgency, at the Third Annual Conference of former secretaries of defense in 1989: "Going forward, we have to make a judgment on what role our country ought to play, and a passive role would be terribly dangerous . . . but who do we want to provide leadership in the world? Somebody else? Name him!"[55] This is how anti-life becomes concrete in the world. The world and human beings living in it are perceived as threat, and the threat must be controlled by those who can demonstrate they are most capable. Domination masquerades as freedom.

FROM IRONIC TO EVIL: WE WERE NEVER INNOCENT

Reinhold Niebuhr, in his poignant analysis of *The Irony of American History* in 1952, described three elements of contemporary history: the "tragic," the "pathetic," and the "ironic." In his own summary, Niebuhr describes the "pathetic" as "suffering caused by purely natural evil," while "the tragic element in a human situation is constituted of conscious choices of evil for the sake of good."[56] Finally, Niebuhr's thick description of the "ironic" element in history is as follows:

> Irony consists of apparently fortuitous incongruities in life which are discovered, upon closer examination, to be not merely fortuitous. . . . A comic situation is proved to be an ironic one if a hidden relation is discovered in the incongruity. If virtue becomes vice through some hidden defect in the virtue; if strength becomes weakness because of the vanity to which strength may prompt the mighty man or nation; if security is transmuted into insecurity because too much reliance is placed upon it; if wisdom becomes folly because it does not know its own limits—in all such cases the situation is ironic.[57]

I include this concept of irony because it describes the way domination can be "hidden" in the guise of virtue, leading to ruin. I have argued that domination masquerades as the American vision of freedom; full spectrum dominance, American sovereignty, and the moral language of good and evil function much like Arendt's analysis of "language rules"; the words do not obscure what is being done, but keeps what is done from being associated with the "old knowledge" of domination.[58] In this way, Donald Rumsfeld and others in the Bush administration could reflect, both to themselves and to the public, on the legend and mythos of the United States as a liberator of Europe from domination in World War II without connecting the work of the global war on terror to the concept of domination. Domination masquerades as freedom. Depending on how much benefit of the doubt one is willing to provide to the

Bush administration, anti-life (domination) masquerading as freedom can closely match Niebuhr's concept of the ironic. That is to say, it all depends on how well domination is a "hidden defect" in the "virtue" of freedom to the planners of the Iraq War themselves—how convinced they actually were that they were advancing the cause of "freedom."

I do not wish to parse out the *intent* of people like Rumsfeld, Bush, Cheney, and others. Anti-life does not depend on explicit intent to wage its assault on life. Their words, actions, and the consequences thereof are enough to demonstrate the logic of anti-life in the global war on terror. Their self-awareness is the key to whether and how deeply they were engaged in evil, and I am not capable of parsing out their level of self-awareness. However, I have no qualms in naming the war they unleashed as an evil work, a project of global domination. I know that of which I am aware, that which was revealed to me through fighting in the war itself—and I can call it nothing but evil. Niebuhr goes on to describe how an ironic situation *must* be dissolved once one becomes aware of the irony:

> The ironic situation is distinguished from a pathetic one by the fact that the person involved in it bears some responsibility for it. It is differentiated from tragedy by the fact that the responsibility is related to an unconscious weakness rather than a conscious resolution. While a pathetic or tragic situation is not dissolved when a person becomes conscious of his involvement in it, an ironic situation must dissolve, if men or nations are made aware of their complicity in it. Such awareness involves some realization of the hidden vanity or pretension by which comedy is turned into irony. This realization either must lead to an abatement of the pretension, which means contrition; or it leads to a desperate accentuation of the vanities to the point where irony turns into pure evil.[59]

The awareness and realization of hidden vanity or pretension, as Niebuhr describes it, parallels the concept of negative revelation I am developing in this book. That this awareness must lead to abatement of the pretension (contrition), I take up in chapter 5; there is a "turning point" (contrition) at which one abandons the orientation of one's life toward war that one has recognized as evil. I became aware, as a young soldier, of my own complicity in working toward global domination, though in my naiveté domination had been "hidden" to me—an incongruity in the "virtue" of freedom. However, once aware of the unfolding of the parasitic premise of domination in the global war on terror, the war itself appeared as "a desperate accentuation of the vanities"; there was nothing comic or ironic left to me in the never-ending war—only pure evil.

That the war appears to me as evil prompts me to push beyond Niebuhr's analysis of the "ironic" in American history. Irony is an incomplete picture of domination's relation to freedom in the global war on terror. Niebuhr's analysis focused on the Cold War relationship between the United States and the Soviet Union. The Soviet Union represented an enemy that had taken certain pretenses of virtue and innocence, pretenses that the United States shared with the Soviet Union, to terrible extremes. That is, the irony in the United States and Soviet relationship is in the fact that both superpowers' pretenses of virtue and innocence obscured an attempt to become "masters of history and destiny." The United States needed to be made aware that in its own confrontation with the Soviet Union, in all the ways the United States was exercising its power to combat the "evils" of communism, the hidden defect of attempting to master and control history itself was obscured. History, like life itself, reveals itself to be "recalcitrant" and resistant to domination and control.[60]

Niebuhr's analysis and critique of the position of the United States is compelling, and perhaps best summarized in the famous last words of the book:

> If we should perish, the ruthlessness of the foe would be only the secondary cause of the disaster. The primary cause would be that the strength of a giant nation was directed by eyes too blind to see all the hazards of the struggle; and the blindness would be induced not by some accident of nature or history but by hatred and vainglory.[61]

These last words, in my view, are the closest Niebuhr gets to describing the situation in which the United States finds itself in the twenty-first century. Nonetheless, Niebuhr still leaves much obscured, even in his own context of mid-twentieth-century America.

Domination is much more than a "hidden defect" in the "virtue" of America's vision of freedom. It is and always has been synonymous with the thing itself. American freedom, while a vision in which some may flourish, is intimately related to the domination, not just of other nations, but of many Americans. James Cone points out a certain blindness in Niebuhr's own work: Niebuhr, along with other progressive white thinkers in the United States, "remained silent about lynching" while "the nightmare in black life continued to deepen."[62] The lynching tree was not some obscured reality or hidden defect while Niebuhr lived; according to Cone, "the lynching tree is the cross in America," and "Niebuhr's focus on realism . . . and the cross . . . should have turned his gaze to the lynching tree."[63] Cone's *The Cross and the Lynching Tree* forces the reader to wrestle with the reality that America's vision of freedom has always come with imperial conquest (especially in the form of slaughtering Native Americans) and domination (especially in the form of attempting to control the black population in America). Reading Cone alongside Niebuhr, Niebuhr's observation that "we were, of course, never as innocent as we pretended to be" takes on a sinister quality. *We were never innocent.* The machinery of full spectrum dominance does not simply fall into our laps. Sovereignty as a way of elevating "American" life while diminishing others cannot be a recent development in order to function so smoothly in the war on terror. The impassioned rhetoric of good versus evil would appear absurd to the public if it were not so deeply lodged in our understanding of who we are. The global war on terror is not an event that begins a new chapter of domination in American history; it is, rather, a continuation and global export of the American "vision" of freedom. The global war on terror is a concrete demonstration of anti-life as a deceptive morality; a project whose ultimate aim is cloaked in the language of goodness, justice, and freedom. Many of us were duped by this morality, orienting our lives toward a goal we thought, in the long run, was about justice in the world. Anti-life masquerades as life. Domination masquerades as American freedom. Life itself is explained and assaulted in the static definitions of good and evil, American and non-American, war and terror.

NOTES

1. George W. Bush. "A Period of Consequences." Speech at The Citadel, Charleston, South Carolina. September 23, 1999, accessed August 3, 2021, http://www3.citadel.edu/pao/addresses/pres_bush.html

2. Hannah Arendt, *The Origins of Totalitarianism*, New Edition with Added Prefaces (New York: Harcourt, Inc., 1994), 326.

3. Donald Rumsfeld, *Known and Unknown: A Memoir* (New York: Sentinel, 2011), 224.

4. George W. Bush. "A Period of Consequences." *Citadel Newsroom, The Citadel,* Charleston South Carolina. September 23, 1999. Accessed August 3, 2021, http://www3.citadel.edu/pao/addresses/pres_bush.html

5. Hannah Arendt, *The Origins of Totalitarianism*, 458–68.

6. Hannah Arendt, *Eichmann in Jerusalem: A Report on the Banality of Evil* (New York: Penguin Books, 2006), 85.

7. Ibid., 85–86.

8. Rumsfeld, *Known and Unknown*, xiv.

9. Donald Rumsfeld, "Department of Defense News Briefing—Secretary Rumsfeld and General Myers." U.S. Department of Defense News Transcript, February 12, 2002, accessed August 3, 2021, https://archive.defense.gov/Transcripts/Transcript.aspx?TranscriptID=2636

10. Rumsfeld, *Known and Unknown*, 719.

11. The direct question to which Rumsfeld was responding: "In regard to Iraq weapons of mass destruction and terrorists, is there any evidence to indicate that Iraq has attempted to or is willing to supply terrorists with weapons of mass destruction? Because there are reports that there is no evidence of a direct link between Baghdad

and some of these terrorist organizations." See Rumsfeld, "Department of Defense News Briefing—Secretary Rumsfeld and General Myers." https://archive.defense.gov/Transcripts/Transcript.aspx?TranscriptID=2636

12. Donald Rumsfeld, *Rumsfeld's Rules: Leadership Lessons in Business, Politics, War, and Life* (New York: Broadside Books, 2013), 107.

13. Bradley Graham, *By His Own Rules: The Ambitions, Successes, and Ultimate Failures of Donald Rumsfeld* (New York: PublicAffairs, 2009), 195–96.

14. Rumsfeld, *Known and Unknown*, 449.

15. Ibid., 297.

16. Ibid., 288.

17. *The Unknown Known*, directed by Errol Morris (Anchor Bay Entertainment, 2014), accessed November 20, 2020, Amazon Prime Video, https://www.amazon.com/Known-Donald-Rumsfeld/dp/B00JGMJ914.

18. Ibid.

19. In a 1983 memo entitled "The Swamp" (referring to the Middle East), Rumsfeld attempted to convey his "sense of the region as a dangerous, shifting place inhospitable to American interests. My initial assessment was that we needed to lighten our hand somewhat in the Middle East, but to proceed carefully so as not to further upset the situation." A key point in the 1983 memo was that U.S. officials "should keep reminding ourselves that it is easier to get into something that it is to get out of it." See Rumsfeld, *Known and Unknown*, 21. For Rumsfeld's recollections about his critique of the Johnson administration and the status of the Vietnam War as a young congressman, see *Known and Unknown*, 69–73.

20. For a more classical exposition of known and unknowns, see Saint Thomas Aquinas, ST I-II, q.76, a. 2. Thomas distinguishes "invincible ignorance" from "vincible ignorance." Invincible ignorance concerns what one is unable to know, because this ignorance "cannot be overcome by study." "Vincible ignorance" can be overcome by study, but it is only considered a sin when it becomes "negligence," that is, when one is ignorant "about matters one is bound to know." In ST I-II, q. 7, a. 8, Thomas gets at a *denial* or *rejection* of knowledge with the category of "affected ignorance"—"as when a man wishes not to know, that he may have an excuse for sin, or that he may not be withheld from sin; according to Job xxi. 14: *We desire not the knowledge of Thy ways.*" St. Thomas Aquinas, *The Summa Theologica of St. Thomas Aquinas: Complete English Edition in Five Volumes*, translated by Fathers of the English Dominican Province, vol. 2 (Notre Dame, IN: Christian Classics, 1981).

21. Rumsfeld, *Known and Unknown*, 202.

22. "Joint Vision 2020: America's Military—Preparing for Tomorrow," *Joint Force Quarterly*, no. 25 (Summer 2000): 57–76.

23. Ibid., 58.

24. Ibid., 61.

25. See "Figure 2. Range of Military Operations" in "Joint Vision 2020," 61.

26. For a robust account of full spectrum dominance with a focus on the outward facing roles of U.S. military chaplains, see Ed Waggoner, *Religion in Uniform: A Critique of U.S. Military Chaplaincy* (New York: Lexington Books, 2019), 103–33.

27. "Joint Vision 2020," 61.

28. Chris Hedges, *War Is a Force That Gives Us Meaning* (New York: Anchor Books, 2003), 148.
29. John Tirman, *The Deaths of Others: The Fate of Civilians in America's Wars* (New York: Oxford University Press, 2011), 193.
30. Rumsfeld, *Known and Unknown*, 600.
31. *Hamdan v. Rumsfeld*, syllabus, 548 U.S. 557 (2006), accessed August 3, 2021, https://www.supremecourt.gov/opinions/05pdf/05-184.pdf
32. Rumsfeld, *Known and Unknown*, 540.
33. Ibid., 540–41.
34. Thomas E. Ricks, *Fiasco: The American Military Adventure in Iraq* (New York: Penguin Books, 2006), 390–412.
35. Ali A. Allawi, *The Occupation of Iraq: Wining the War, Losing the Peace* (New Haven, CT: Yale University Press, 2007), 287.
36. Ricks, *Fiasco*, 195.
37. Ibid., 224, 238.
38. It is worth noting that cordon and sweep operations, focused on detention and interrogation, were not accepted as best practice by all U.S. military commanders in Iraq. For examples, see the 101st Airborne under the command of David Petraeus in 2003–2004. See Ricks, *Fiasco*, 228–32.
39. Dexter Filkins, *The Forever War* (New York: Vintage Books, 2009), 122–23.
40. George W. Bush. "A Period of Consequences." Speech at the Citadel, Charleston, South Carolina. September 23, 1999, accessed August 3, 2021, http://www3.citadel.edu/pao/addresses/pres_bush.html
41. George W. Bush, "Commencement Address at the United States Military Academy in West Point, New York," *Weekly Compilation of Presidential Documents* 38, no. 2 (June 10, 2002): 944–48.
42. George W. Bush, "Commencement Address at . . . West Point."
43. Donald Rumsfeld, "Sovereignty and Anticipatory Self-Defense." OSD Policy, August 24, 2002, accessed August 3, 2021, https://www.rumsfeld.com/archives
44. Ibid.
45. United States. *The National Security Strategy of the United States of America* (Washington, DC: President of the U.S., 2002), accessed August 3, 2021, https://georgewbush-whitehouse.archives.gov/nsc/nss/2002/. See especially section V: Prevent Our Enemies from Threatening Us, Our Allies, and Our Friends with Weapons of Mass Destruction.
46. *Military Commissions Act of 2006*, Public Law 109-366, *U.S. Statutes at Large* 120 (2006): 2600–2637. See especially section 948b., "No alien unlawful enemy combatant subject to trial by military commission under this chapter may invoke the Geneva Conventions as a source of rights," accessed August 3, 2021, https://www.loc.gov/rr/frd/Military_Law/pdf/PL-109-366.pdf
47. See Rumsfeld, *Known and Unknown*, 557, 561–64, 588–90; Graham, *By His Own Rules*, 316–22; Ricks, *Fiasco*, 292, 297.
48. Rumsfeld, *Known and Unknown*, 600.
49. Ricks, *Fiasco*, 281.

50. The Department of Defense regularly updates these numbers, identified by specific campaigns in the global war on terror, at "Casualty Status," accessed August 3, 2021, https://dod.defense.gov/News/Casualty-Status/

51. Secretary Donald H. Rumsfeld, interview by Tony Snow, *Fox News Sunday*, November 2, 2003, accessed August 3, 2021, https://archive.defense.gov/Transcripts/Transcript.aspx?TranscriptID=2870. A version of this statement, "We don't do body counts," is often attributed to General Tommy Franks at Bagram Air Base in Afghanistan in March 2002. I have quoted Rumsfeld rather than Franks because the DoD kept thorough transcripts of Rumsfeld's briefings, and he has been at the center of my argument in this chapter. Versions of the statement are repeated in various briefings by Bush administration officials throughout the war on terror.

52. For example, "Iraq Body Count," accessed August 3, 2021, https://www.iraqbodycount.org/, focusing on confirmed deaths reported in English news reports, gives a bare minimum range between 185,395 and 208,419 for civilian deaths. Physicians for Social Responsibility, after evaluating several studies on Iraqi deaths, concluded that "the war has, directly or indirectly, killed around 1 million people in Iraq." See Physicians for Social Responsibility, *Body Count: Casualty Figures after 10 years of the "War on Terror:" Iraq, Afghanistan, Pakistan*, First International Edition (Washington, DC, 2015), 14. See also "Iraq: The Human Cost" website hosted by MIT: http://web.mit.edu/humancostiraq/ and UNHCR's Iraq "Global Focus": http://reporting.unhcr.org/node/2547 regarding the millions displaced by the war.

53. C.J. Chivers, *The Fighters: Americans in Combat in Afghanistan and Iraq* (New York: Simon and Schuster, 2018), xxii.

54. George W. Bush, "Commencement Address at the United States Military Academy in West Point, New York," *Weekly Compilation of Presidential Documents* 38, no. 2 (June 10, 2002): 944–48.

55. "The Third Annual Report of the Secretaries of Defense," Georgia Public Television (1989), accessed via YouTube August 3, 2021, https://www.youtube.com/watch?v=9fPzvG7qFRI

56. Reinhold Niebuhr, *The Irony of American History* (Chicago: University of Chicago Press, 2008), xxiii.

57. Ibid., xxiv.

58. Arendt, *Eichmann in Jerusalem*, 85–86.

59. Niebuhr, *The Irony of American History*, xxiv.

60. See especially "Chapter IV: The Master of Destiny," in Niebuhr, *Irony of American History*, 65–88.

61. Niebuhr, *Irony of American History*, 174.

62. James H. Cone, *The Cross and the Lynching Tree* (Maryknoll, NY: Orbis Books, 2011), 49.

63. Cone, *The Cross and The Lynching Tree*, 38, 158. See Chapter 2, Cone's reflection on Reinhold Niebuhr, for a more thorough analysis of Niebuhr on race and class in America.

Chapter 3

Moral Injury as Negative Revelation, Part I

"Moral"—Betrayed by Convention

War reveals something to those who are immersed in it. The revelation is negative; one senses with a unique clarity what is not there—or perhaps it is better to say, one senses that which has been obscured, distorted, hidden by anti-life. In Tim O'Brien's words, "In the midst of evil you want to be a good man. You want decency. You want justice, courtesy and human concord . . . filled with a hard, aching love for how the world could be and always should be, but now is not."[1] Goodness, justice, freedom—all those things for which politicians and power holders claim going to war is necessary—are revealed in war as almost perfectly absent. In this way, war is a condition like Simone Weil's "affliction";[2] that which one most longs for is felt as most distant. The content of this negative revelation through an almost perfect absence has to do with goodness itself—life itself. In the trajectory of this book, it is coming to an awareness that anti-life has masqueraded as life; the language of goodness has been emptied from the inside, now used as a cloak for domination. The effect of this revelation on the individual who is immersed in war brings about another awareness concerning the self who has sought to do the good and failed. The negative revelation in its most simple two-fold form: "The world is not what I thought it was/wanted it to be; and, I am not who I thought I was/wanted to be."

To this point, I have shown in chapter 1 how anti-life poses as life, becoming a "morality" that dupes us. In terms of the negative revelation: I thought I was fighting for life, but I was dealing death. In chapter 2, I more specifically applied the concept of anti-life to the U.S.-led global war on terror, in which domination disguises itself in the "American vision of freedom." In the introduction, I cited Origen, who argued with other ancient theologians and philosophers that he felt held a mistaken view of goodness and justice: "they think that justice is to do evil to the evil and good to the good; that is, according to their meaning, that one who is just will not show himself well disposed to the evil, but will behave towards them with a kind of hatred."[3] I am claiming that something is awry with how we think of goodness and justice in the United States.

In this chapter and the following one, I rework the concept of moral injury as negative revelation. Much literature on moral injury focuses on individuals: their actions, their values, their traumatic experiences, and how they recover or do not recover from trauma. In my view, the focus on individuals is due to the fact that a vast amount of the discourse on moral injury comes from the medical community—people focused on helping and treating individual U.S. veterans who deal with intense feelings of anger, despair, guilt, and shame. This focus on the individual has been important and valuable work. I split my treatment of moral injury into chapters because I do not wish to disregard the suffering of individuals, which will be my focus in chapter 4.

While I think there is much value in the current literature on moral injury, the focus on individuals and individual actions/events leaves me dissatisfied with the term. I am dissatisfied with the term "moral injury" because it often brackets, delays, or obscures theological and ethical questions about war. For me, the war itself is the ultimate transgression and betrayal in which all other individual transgressions and betrayals in literature are immersed. Providing a more complete account of moral injury requires providing a more robust account of the war itself and how war is valued in U.S. society.

In the first section of this chapter, I provide a brief survey of moral injury literature, focusing specifically on questions of morality and what, in my view, the literature leaves out regarding these questions. In the second section, I take aim at "moral convention" with an analysis of just war theory. I am arguing that moral convention has betrayed people. This is a layer of moral injury I am adding to the insights already provided by much moral injury literature regarding the pain and suffering resulting in an individual betraying moral commitments. With my attention to just war theory, I am also arguing that something has gone wrong in a much broader sense regarding how Americans think of "what's right." For clarity, I will make a broad and general claim here, to be nuanced in the pages to follow: many Americans value and respect the military as an institution. In my view, Americans trust or hope that when the U.S. military is deployed around the world and using force, it is to bring about some form of peace and/or justice. This is captured in the adage "peace through strength," echoing from the ancient Romans through contemporary U.S. foreign policy. While many Americans are perhaps not familiar with the intricacies of just war theory, they do know that there are rules and principles that must be followed. I am arguing that what has always been wrong about the global war on terror is at the heart of just war theory: if the principles of just war are to function at all, soldiers on both sides of a conflict should be treated as "moral equals."[4] Our enemies in this war have not been treated as moral equals; rather, they have been treated with "a kind of hatred," objects of domination. Hatred is not justice.

This chapter is my analysis of how deeply and concretely anti-life as a kind of hatred corrupts the concepts of goodness and justice in war. This hatred, this treating of others as objects of domination, is not only a break with just war theory, but it is also a break with how many Americans want to believe their government and their military is behaving in the world. To be clear, I am talking still talking about a "morality" that dupes us. Anti-life is insidious. As I take aim at "moral convention" in the chapter, as a betrayer of human beings, I am talking about how a hatred of others creeps into both the ethics of war and a broader set of social values in the United States, posing as goodness and justice.

I grew up reading Stephen King novels, who was inspired by the work of H. P. Lovecraft. Both writers have mastered the art of horror in storytelling. I am not attempting to tell a Lovecraftian story—though there are some similarities. Lovecraft's tales offer glimpses behind a cosmic curtain—characters in his stories see just a sliver of the cosmos beyond our reality, a cosmos populated by sinister beings for whom the lives of human beings do not register. Lovecraft's characters often go mad after receiving this glimpse of unfiltered cosmic reality. In a similar way, I have used the concept of anti-life to argue that underneath political and social conceptions of goodness and justice, domination and a kind of hatred go about concealed. War offers a glimpse of that domination and hatred. Madness and despair may result. However, domination and hatred do not constitute reality. I am challenging the facade of goodness, justice, and the American ideal of "freedom" in order to find a glimpse of goodness beyond anti-life, not to claim that anti-life is all that remains underneath the masquerade.

My own negative revelation in war peeled back multiple curtains for me. The first curtain was the mistaken view of goodness and justice described in chapter 2. In war, I felt domination rather than freedom. Domination was the poison revealed to me in what I thought was goodness. The antidote cannot comprise putting the curtain back in place, wrapping myself in the rhetoric of anti-life that led me to war in the first place. The antidote is to dig deeper still, underneath the second curtain of anti-life. In chapter 2, I noted the ways domination and dehumanization function underneath the language of full spectrum dominance, sovereignty, and moral superiority. A negative revelation in war strips away that language. One comes face to face with anti-life without a disguise. The experience of an "aching love for the way the world could be and always should be, but now is not"[5] is not a desire for new assumptions and presuppositions to help one cope with anti-life—it is longing for life itself. The desire for life, in its near perfect absence (in the midst of anti-life), tears a hole through the curtain of anti-life. That which is revealed is fragile, uncertain, and flickering. It is potentiality, spontaneity, surprise. It is mystery. It is life that cannot be negated by anti-life.

INTRODUCING MORAL INJURY

War rips away assumptions and presuppositions: "The world is not what I thought it was/wanted it to be; and, I am not who I thought I was/wanted to be." The term "moral injury" captures both aspects of the negative revelation in war distilled into two words: moral + injury. I have put this observation even more briefly elsewhere: "moral injury is despair of the world and oneself."[6] The negative revelation of moral injury is a pit of despair, but the mystery of life is also in the pit. The recognition of world and self not as they should and could be offers the ground to imagine a different world and different self.

Literature on moral injury is expanding rapidly in several disciplines. In this chapter and the next, I offer my own framing of the term as a concrete encounter with anti-life in the guise of life. This chapter will focus on the first half of the term, the "moral," while chapter 4 focuses on the "injury." In my framework of moral injury as despair of world and self, moral corresponds to world and injury corresponds to self. Before reviewing the concept of moral injury, I first turn to literature to put a life in front of us. As Martha Nussbaum posits, "a novel, just because it is not our life, places us in a moral position that is favorable for perception and it shows us what it would be like to take up that position in life."[7] In his novel *The Yellow Birds*, Kevin Powers presents a thick description of moral injury without using the term. The main character in Powers's novel, Private Bartle, is home after a tour in Iraq, and is watching some of his old friends party across the river from where he sits and wonders what it would be like to speak to them:

Why didn't I just wade out to them? What would I say? "Hey, how are you?"

[. . .] Or should I have said that I wanted to die, not in the sense of wanting to throw myself off that train bridge over there, but more like wanting to be asleep forever because there isn't any making up for killing women or even watching women get killed [. . .] and it was like just trying to kill everything you saw sometimes because it felt like there was acid seeping down into your soul and then your soul is gone and knowing from being taught your whole life that there is no making up for what you are doing [. . .] but then even your mother is so happy and proud because you lined up your sight posts and made people crumple [. . .] and then that thing you started to notice slipping away is gone and now it's becoming inverted, like you have bottomed out in your spirit but yet a deeper hole is being dug because everybody is so fucking happy to see you, the murderer, the fucking accomplice, the at-bare-minimum bearer of some fucking responsibility, and everyone wants to slap you on the back and you start to want to burn the whole goddamn country down, you want to burn every goddamn yellow ribbon in sight, and you can't explain it but it's just, like, Fuck you, but then you signed up to go so it's all your fault, really, because you went on purpose, so you are in the end doubly fucked.[8]

Moral injury is the position of being "doubly fucked."

In Private Bartle's stream of consciousness, there is the initial self-condemnation—knowing that he has done things for which there is "no making up" and knowing that this is something for which he volunteered. The deeper violation is that everyone back home is grateful and happy to see him. That which is poisoning him is celebrated by his family and culture. Because he "went on purpose," the truth he might tell about this despair remains a stream of consciousness. He is doubly fucked. He is not who he thought he was or who he wanted to be—and he is the only one who knows this truth. This is one facet of moral injury. However, the other facet is the world—the world of home, the world of morality which raised Bartle to know that he could never make up for killing and yet celebrates his killing of others. This is morality poisoned by anti-life, and it is this aspect of moral injury's double-fucking that is the focus of this chapter.

For all the burgeoning research on moral injury in recent years, the concept of moral injury is intimately tied to the everyday language regarding the difference between right and wrong. The commonsense assumption of the difference between right and wrong cannot be set aside as simple or self-evident. I argue that moral injury results from a moral convention that betrays human beings. The moral convention is a social construction involving the difference between right and wrong, and my investigation of this particular kind of betrayal must begin with an investigation of this difference at work in the convention.

I am using the term "moral convention" in a specific way, which demands some explanation here. Brian Stiltner provides a clear distinction between ethics and morality: "*Ethics* is associated with formal analysis, academic study, and social and professional codes of conduct. *Morality*, on the other hand, is associated with one's personal living based upon values"; Stiltner continues, citing Vincent Genovesi, "'morality' is what we live, whereas 'ethics' is what we study."[9] It is also germane to distinguish "normative" and "applied" ethics; normative ethics are theories providing "basic guidelines for ethical action in any context, whereas applied ethics are working out those norms to fit concrete situations and contexts."[10] As I use the term "moral convention," I am referring to what we live *and* what we study, and I am referring to ethical norms *and* concrete applications. By using the term "moral convention," I am arguing that ethical norms and standards become conflated and confused with what we *live*; principles and life are flattened together—diminishing both.

For example, many Americans felt legitimate moral outrage at the murder of civilians when the World Trade Center was attacked and destroyed. The outrage comes from what we live, a rejection of the murder of innocents as wrong. The rejection of murder can also be framed in principle, through the application of ethical norms. However, George W. Bush froze that moment of moral outrage in stasis, describing the United States in "a conflict between good and evil."[11] This position of moral superiority conflates norms and living. If we are fighting an opponent that is in principle evil, then the way we live out the fighting must be good and just; or vice versa, the opponent we are fighting must be evil, because we who are good are the ones fighting them. Life and principle are conflated, reduced. Humans are made into superhuman paragons of goodness fighting against subhuman agents of evil. Moral convention, a fabric to help us discern the rightness and wrongness of specific actions, is caught up in and reifies the artifice. Moral injury, as I describe it in this chapter, is the recognition of a moral convention as anti-life.

Moral Injury and Convention from the Perspective of Clinicians

Jonathan Shay is credited with coining the term "moral injury" after years of working with Vietnam veterans in a Veterans Affairs Outpatient Clinic in Boston. Shay begins his landmark work, *Achilles in Vietnam*: "We begin in the moral world of the soldier—what his [sic] culture understands to be right."[12] Shay clearly defines what he means by using the term "what's right": "No single English word takes in the whole sweep of a culture's definition of right and wrong; we use terms such as moral order, convention, normative expectations, ethics, and commonly understood social values. The ancient Greek word that Homer used, *thémis*, encompasses all these meanings."[13]

When *thémis* or "what's right" is betrayed, according to Shay, Achilles and modern soldiers alike respond and react with some form of *mênis* or "indignant rage."[14] This response of indignant rage is described in the subtitle of Shay's work as "the undoing of character." In his second book, Shay uses these concepts as the foundation for his definition of moral injury: "the betrayal of 'what's right' in a high stakes situation by someone who holds power."[15]

When Shay first turned to Homer's *Iliad* to flesh out his concept of "betrayal of 'what's right,'" the first example he provided was "Agamémnon's seizure of Achilles' woman"; the woman Brisêis was a "prize of honor [. . .] voted by the troops for Achilles' valor in combat."[16] For Shay, the importance of the illustration is not to question whether the woman *should* have been viewed as a prize of war; rather, it is that Achilles, the other soldiers, Achilles's mother—virtually everyone at the scene—clearly understands that Agamémnon violated "what's right" with respect to Achilles. Shay's account of moral injury leaves one with no ground to challenge "what's right" itself— to say that taking a woman as a war-prize is, in itself, *wrong*. All one can say here is that Agamémnon betrayed convention; I argue that we must be able to go further, we must be able to say that convention betrayed Brisêis.

"What's right" (*thémis*) is a kind of place-holder concept in Shay's work. It changes over time and is highly subjective, defined locally and having to do with social consent. "What's right" does not necessarily mean "what's *right*" (in the sense that there is an absolute, unchanging definition of rightness); for something to count as "what's right," it simply needs to be commonly understood as such. The absolute or universal quality of "what's right" has to do with its betrayal. For Shay, "what's right" is defined by a particular group or community (this changes over time); when it is betrayed, rage and social withdrawal ensue (this does not change over time). Shay claims: "Veterans can usually recover from horror, fear, and grief once they return to civilian life, so long as "what's right" has not also been violated."[17] Shay begins his work with the "whole sweep of a culture's definition of right and wrong," or *thémis*, but leaves *thémis* itself unexamined except to speak of its betrayal by power holders. Shay's work on moral injury is invaluable, in my view. However, this passing over of the difference between right and wrong is a critical gap—a leap from the premise of "what's right" to the conclusion of its betrayal.

The sweep of a whole culture may provide a robust account of right and wrong, but this does not preclude the whole culture from getting the whole thing wrong—either in theory or in practice.

In a landmark 2009 article in *Clinical Psychology Review*, Brett Litz and a team of other scholars and clinicians provided another working definition of moral injury: "the lasting psychological, biological, spiritual, behavioral, and social impact of perpetrating, failing to prevent, bearing witness to, or learning about acts that transgress deeply held moral beliefs and expectations." [18] The team's definition of "morals" closely resembles Shay's "what's right": "Morals are defined as the personal and shared familial, cultural, societal, and legal rules for social behavior, either tacit or explicit. Morals are fundamental assumptions about how things should work and how one should behave in the world."[19]

The basic distinction between Shay's definition and the definition offered by Litz et al. is the question of *who does the betraying*. In Shay's own words:

"In their definition the violator is the self, whereas in mine the violator is a powerholder [. . . in their definition] moral injury arises when a service member does something in war that violates *their own* ideals, ethics, or attachments."[20] The distinction Shay highlights in the newer definition is its greatest strength. The acknowledgment that the self can do the betraying rather than a legitimate authority provides a much-needed expansion to Shay's definition. Authorities and power holders do not hold a monopoly over betrayal.

Moreover, morality itself is expanded and nuanced in the Litz et al. definition. For example, in Shay's case of Agamemnon and Achilles, the "what's right" that is betrayed is the same across the board—it is "what's right" because it is commonly understood by the individuals present. Litz et al. keep the social valence of morality while also including "fundamental assumptions about how things should work and how one should behave in the world," which can be shaped at both a *personal* and *familial* level. Simply put, the second definition opens the possibility that there are multiple "moralities" at play in a given context. The soldier on the battlefield indeed shares a common understanding of "what's right" with her partners in arms, but she also has her own "deeply held moral beliefs and expectations." Those deeply held moral beliefs and expectations may or may not be shared by other soldiers. They can be formed and internalized in contexts she does not hold in common with other soldiers.[21]

Ultimately, however, "morality" or "what's right," even when nuanced in the second definition, remains a place-holder concept. There is an underlying assumption in both definitions that "what's right" or "deeply held moral beliefs and expectations," so long as they are not violated, are themselves not problematic. In other words, there is tacit validation that "what's right" is, in fact, right. My primary critique of Shay and Litz's definitions is that one can act consistently out of a common understanding of "what's right," even out of one's "deeply held moral convictions," *without violating them*—and moral injury can still occur.[22] The moral convention, in both definitions, is that which is betrayed—whether it resides in the sweep of a whole culture or is embedded in an individual's own deeply held beliefs. To be clear, Shay, Litz, and others have provided invaluable work on moral injury. Rule breaking, betraying one's conscience, and being manipulated/coerced into breaking rules or going against one's conscience *are injurious*. The betrayal of moral convention is an important definition of moral injury. In the excerpt from *The Yellow Birds* above, Private Bartle hates himself for what he has done—what he has been raised to know there is "no making up for." What Bartle has done constitutes a betrayal of what's right, a deeply held moral conviction—this is what constitutes moral injury in the work of Shay and Litz et al.

I do not wish to replace the definitions provided by the medical community, nor do I wish to disparage the work the medical community is doing.

They are helping a population cope with and heal from the psychic and spiritual pain resulting from war. Without the hard work done by these clinicians and researchers, most of this population sent to war by their own government would be left to deal with their pain in isolation. Also, to be sure, clinicians are well aware of the important questions of morality and ethics.[23] However, I am positing another layer of moral injury in which *people* are betrayed by a moral convention of anti-life. To posit this deeper layer, I am making claims clinicians, qua clinicians, are hesitant to make. Focusing solely on the work of Litz et al., Warren Kinghorn argues that the disciplinary context of clinicians places limits on what can be said of morality: "They cannot pass judgment on the validity of the moral rules and assumptions that individual soldiers carry, since to do so would be to venture into the ethics of war. They also cannot name any deeper reality that moral assumptions and the rules that engender them might reflect."[24] I am passing judgment on rules and assumptions, venturing into the ethics of war, and I am attempting to name a deeper reality.[25] The moral convention undergirding the global war on terror is poisoned by anti-life. While many in the United States have now come to criticize the war, the war goes on. The moral convention driving it is healthy and thriving. To borrow from Kevin Powers's novel again, "everybody is so fucking happy to see you, the murderer, the fucking accomplice, the at-bare-minimum bearer of some fucking responsibility."[26] This is the position of being "doubly fucked"—to continue to see what's wrong celebrated as what's right.

WHAT'S WRONG WITH "WHAT'S RIGHT"

I want to push beyond the medical constructions of moral injury to critically analyze what constitutes the "moral." I am not the first to do this. According to Tyler Boudreau, a former Marine officer, "what's most useful about the term "moral injury" is that it takes the problem out of the hands of the mental health profession and the military and attempts to place it where it belongs—in society, in the community, and in the family—precisely where moral questions should be posed and wrangled with."[27] Boudreau goes on to name the heart of the problem resulting from moral injury construed solely as a medical concept:

> Nobody wants to talk about the Iraqis. It's always about *the troops*. But "moral injury" by definition includes the memories of those who have been harmed. Without the Iraqi people, the troops can have no moral injuries to speak of. And the only way Americans can fathom the meaning of this term, "moral injury," is to acknowledge the humanity of the Iraqis.[28]

To put Boudreau's observations in the words of my own work, anti-life assumes and dehumanizes an "enemy" in the Iraqi other. Moral injury is, in part, a recognition that this dehumanization of the "enemy" has occurred, and that the dehumanization is reified and celebrated at home. Locating moral injury in the individual U.S. military veteran as a quasi-medical diagnosis obscures that revelation. Moreover, it dehumanizes the veteran herself, making her a patient with a problem whereas she is in fact a human with an insight. Moral injury as a diagnostic term can itself be co-opted by anti-life, leaving one "doubly fucked"—not able to speak substantively of the harm that was done to others while simultaneously becoming a mental health problem in the eyes of the institutions that supported the harm of others.

Joseph Wiinikka-Lydon, a contemporary ethicist, calls moral injury a "visceral experience of policy, as well as cultural assumptions, that are put into effect corporately on the ground through the bodies of soldiers and others."[29] Wiinikka-Lydon also draws on Boudreau's story, naming moral injury as grounds for potential "prophetic insight, understanding prophetic as seeing deeply and radically into the truth of the present and how one's country is actually affecting others throughout the world."[30] What is true in Boudreau's account of moral injury is true in the fictional account of Private Bartle. Seeing deeply and radically into the truth is to see *people* overrun and destroyed by anti-life, to see anti-life enshrined as goodness in one's own society.[31]

Martha Nussbaum on *Nomos*

Jonathan Shay, in his treatment of *thémis* and its betrayal in *Achilles in Vietnam*, draws heavily on Martha Nussbaum's *The Fragility of Goodness*. Shay's treatment of the *Iliad* parallels a trajectory that had already been developed by Nussbaum's treatment of Euripides's *Hecuba*, that is, the undoing of character. In Shay's work, convention (*thémis*) is betrayed, sending Achilles into a violent rage which leads to the undoing of his character. Shay's primary contribution was to recognize this undoing of character unfolding in the lives of the Vietnam veterans he treated.[32]

We also find betrayal of convention leading to the undoing of character in Martha Nussbaum's reading of *Hecuba*, which focuses on the concept of *nomos*.[33] In the play, both of Hecuba's children die, but it is the death of her son, Polydorous, at the hands of Polymestor, once Hecuba's friend, that leads to Hecuba's "metamorphosis," the deformation of her character into something like a "dog."[34] According to Nussbaum, there are two critical keys for understanding Hecuba's undoing, and both are related to Hecuba's understanding of good character: "First, the social and relational nature of her central value commitments, her reliance upon fragile things; second, her anthropocentricity: her belief that ethical commitments are human things, backed by nothing harder or more stable."[35] Nussbaum continues, summarizing Hecuba's conception of *nomos*: "Deep human agreements (or practices) concerning value are the ultimate authority for moral norms. If "convention" is wiped out, there is no higher tribunal to which we can appeal. Even the gods exist only within this human world."[36] The moral convention, for Hecuba, is a human construction, but it is a sturdy construct; and, it is all human beings have for determining the difference between right and wrong. It is built relationally, through agreement. When Polymestor murders Hecuba's son, Polydorous, he betrays the deeply relational and human moral convention of *nomos*; in response to the betrayal, Hecuba is undone, much like Achilles is undone in the *Iliad*. This is the type of moral injury most studied in current literature on the topic: what's right is betrayed/transgressed, either by oneself or by another, resulting in enduring psychic/emotional/spiritual trauma.

Nussbaum provides another layer of the story beyond the undoing of character in response to betrayed moral convention. It is not just Hecuba who is revealed as fragile; *nomos* itself is fragile and can be destroyed. In the play, Polymestor and Hecuba, as *xenos* ("guest friend") and *philos* ("loved one"), "are bound by the most binding tie that exists by *nomos*, the tie that most fundamentally indicates one human's openness to another, his [*sic*] willingness to join with that other in a common moral world."[37] Betrayal of *nomos* does not fully describe the murder of Polydorous by Polymestor. The murder is a revelation to Hecuba that "the *nomoi* that structured her world never were, for this beloved other party, binding *nomoi*. [. . .] If this best and deepest case of human social value has proven [. . .] untrustworthy, then nothing is ever entirely deserving of my trust."[38] Nussbaum calls this event "a dislocation, a rending of the world," bringing a feeling of "complete disorder, lack of structure."[39] Polymestor's betrayal of Hecuba depended on Hecuba's trust in *nomos*, in moral convention. There is a double betrayal here; Hecuba is betrayed by Polymestor, and she is betrayed by her trust in the moral convention itself.

The rest of Nussbaum's treatment of *Hecuba* develops how Hecuba replaces the old *nomos* of trust with a new *nomos* of distrust, characterized by revenge: "Hecuba makes the world over in the image of the possibility of non-relation, the possibility knowledge of which destroyed her trust . . . a world of splendid security and splendid isolation."[40] Again, there are parallels with Achilles in the *Iliad*. What I wish to highlight from Nussbaum's work is not the deformation of one person's character brought about by another person's betrayal of moral convention, but rather the malleable and fickle quality of moral convention itself. I do not deny that the betrayal of moral convention by one person in relation to another can bring about disastrous consequences. Shay and Nussbaum both describe this process in richly nuanced ways.

Nussbaum, however, puts before us the possibility of moral convention itself as untrustworthy. Moreover, through Hecuba's restructuring of her world by replacing one *nomos* with another, Nussbaum presents a world in which a moral convention of revenge sprouts from and devours a moral convention of relationality.

Personally Experiencing the Convention

When I was nineteen years old, I got on a plane and flew to Iraq—an enlisted Army soldier, part of "Operation Iraqi Freedom II." I spent my six months in Iraq driving around the city of Baghdad; as an explosive ordnance disposal technician, I was to help remove or destroy explosive threats—mainly to protect other U.S. military forces. I drove with aggression; I carried a weapon; I shouted and cursed; I was sometimes on site when people were taken from their homes to be placed in detention indefinitely. I had pocket-sized "Rules of Engagement" that I carried with me; I knew how to treat an enemy, when to engage and when not to engage. None of this would have taken place if I had not, when I was seventeen years old, sworn to defend the U.S. Constitution from threats both foreign and domestic. I was not sure what that oath meant at the time, and I am still not certain that I know.

What I do know: none of those things I did or witnessed in Iraq were a betrayal of convention. When I compare my story to the stories of other veterans who were there at the time, all the main elements are par for the course. They were to be expected, part of "what was right" in the situation. Nevertheless, I cannot help but look back at that time and feel that it was all *wrong*. Why is this so, and who is to blame? There are choices for assigning blame and responsibility for the feeling of wrongness, each true in part. I can blame myself; I can blame the Army; I can blame the Bush administration; I can blame "terrorists"; I can blame indifferent U.S. citizens. Each of these is worth a book length treatment. What I wish to take aim at here is moral convention.

If I am right to say that nothing that happened during my stay in Iraq betrayed convention, and that all that happened there nevertheless feels wrong—how am I to come to terms with the concept a shared moral world? There is something *wrong* with "what's right." I posit that there are two possibilities for describing what's wrong with "what's right." The first possibility is to say that there are, in fact, two robust moral conventions at play when a nation goes to war. There is a moral convention at home, and a moral convention at war—and these two are distinct and exclusive. That is to say, in war it is expected that I wear armor, shoot at enemies, blow things up, and treat most civilians with suspicion; this is *not* expected at home. The warfighter here leaves one convention and adopts another while she is at war; she returns home and leaves the war convention behind her. The other possibility is to say that there is one moral convention at work—a moral convention in which peace and security at home is always in a symbiotic relationship with war and chaos abroad. The peace at home and the war abroad each draw benefits from the other. In this case, the moral convention is split in two; the only ones who see both halves of the symbiotic relationship at work are the ones who go to war. It is this second possibility, the symbiotic moral convention, that I argue is at work and betraying human beings. Taking both halves together, the moral convention defining "what's right" regarding the United States in relation to the rest of the world is revealed as anti-life.

It is the moral convention as symbiotic that captures my feeling of wrongness and being betrayed by convention, but the betrayal is made possible only with the assumption of two distinct moral conventions: that peace and security at home is a permanent, stable reality that is only temporally interrupted by its defense in war. If I can say anything about my oath to defend the Constitution, it is captured by the assumption that I could become a soldier and fight a war—switching from *the* moral convention, all the appropriate expectations, guidelines, and behaviors that comprised "home"—to a *temporary* moral convention of war. The assumption was that I could do this all without disrupting my perception of the world and the moral convention through which I was related to family, friends, loved ones, and other citizens.

What happened in Iraq was a "rending of the world"; a revelation that the moral convention, as I had understood it, was untrustworthy. It was a revelation that I did not enter into a moral convention of war that was distinct from the moral convention operating at home, but that the moral convention of "home" supported, depended on, and included war. The world was not what I had thought it was—the world both at home and Iraq was always a world at war. The moral convention had not been betrayed; it had operated like a well-oiled machine. The moral convention was the betrayer.

Just War Theory and the Moral Convention

The reader may or may not agree with me regarding the plausibility of a symbiotic moral convention. Social scientist and philosopher Michael Walzer would likely object to what I have proposed. However, Walzer does draw a sharp distinction between moral expectations in war and moral expectations at home: "wars and battles are not 'cases' to which the law and morality of everyday life can be applied; by definition, they don't take place in civil society."[41] Walzer argues that there is a *"moral reality of war* [. . .] the truth is that one of the things most of us want, even in war, is to act or to seem to act morally. And we want that, most simply, because we know what morality means (at least, we know what it is generally thought to mean)."[42]

The moral reality of war, in Walzer's view, constitutes a "war convention" (the *jus in bello* category of just war theory) and that convention "must first be morally plausible to large numbers of men and women; it must correspond to our sense of what is right."[43] There are two principles of the war convention: first, "once war has begun, soldiers are subject to attack at any time (unless they are wounded or captured"; second, "noncombatants cannot be attacked at any time."[44] It is critical to note that this convention is only in play *once war has begun*. The war convention, according to Walzer, "sets the terms of a moral condition that comes into existence only when armies of victims meet. [. . .] The convention accepts that victimization or at least assumes it, and starts from there."[45] Walzer acknowledges that noncombatants are, in fact, often killed in war, and he provides a strict reinterpretation of the old principle of "double effect" (the principle that allows that some legitimate military actions result in unintended "evils," namely, the death of noncombatants), adding that the combatant must show "some sign of a positive commitment to save civilian lives," even at "costs to himself [*sic*]."[46]

In my view, Walzer gives the theory of a just war its best articulation, especially regarding the principle of double effect. However, Walzer's work immediately begs the question: what does a "civilian life" entail? Is one not a victim of war so long as one can go on breathing? A civilian's bare life may be saved; however, her home might still be destroyed, her family displaced or placed in an unknown detention cell, her workplace demolished, her government reduced to shambles, the roads she travels reduced to rubble. This was the "freedom" the U.S. military provided, from my perspective, in "Operation Iraqi Freedom II." When we accept the first principle of the war convention, the victimization of armies, we implicitly accept with it the victimization of a multitude of others. The convention betrays because it begins from a false premise that war begins and ends. In fact, war and war's victimization of people goes on and on, and war will "have its way."[47]

Robert Meagher claims that "just war theory is a dead letter," that it never delivered on its promises of "the possibility of war without sin, [. . .] criminality [. . .] guilt or shame."[48] Taking a stab at the war convention, Meagher goes on to say, "On paper, just war was to be all about proportionality and fair play. What made it irrelevant was that it just didn't describe war. War has its own rules, and they don't include fair play, moral limits, or an agreement that right trumps might."[49] Meagher goes too far, in my view, to claim that the theory is "irrelevant." Walzer, for instance, makes a strong case that "the transformation of war into a political struggle has as its prior condition the restraint of war as a military struggle [. . .] we must begin by insisting upon the rules of war and by holding soldiers rigidly to the norms they set."[50] Walzer takes the world we live in quite seriously; and, if war continues to unfold in our midst, we need people like Walzer to articulate a theory of war at its best—that is, war and its consequences restrained as much as possible.

What needs to be recalled here is a distinction between ethics and morals, what we study and what we live. Again, Walzer articulates the best ethics, or *study* of war. Meagher's claim about the irrelevance of just war theory regards how war is *lived*. I do not feel betrayed by Walzer's ethics of a just war. I feel betrayed by a moral convention—a conflation of the theory of war fought rightly and war as it appears in actuality, when "armies of victims" collide and leave countless victims in their wake. What I mean by a "moral convention" of war is that which betrays soldiers at war and citizens at home alike. I posit that because we can articulate how a war *should* be fought, we often assume that war to some extent unfolds that way in reality. To be clear, I am not accusing Walzer of this conflation. I am suggesting that the conflation exists and is alive and thriving in an everyday symbiotic moral convention. We do not treat our "enemies" as our moral equals.

I agree with Meagher that just war theory does not describe war; however, this does not render the theory irrelevant. I agree with Walzer that we can indeed think of war as a moral reality that makes sense. The conflation and betrayal that I am pointing to is this: we can too easily assume and imagine that the war described in theory—war as it *should* be fought if it must be—is the war that actually *takes place*. There is a short-circuit at work; the norms outlined by Walzer must be applied and enforced in concrete situations. What I argue is happening, on the contrary, is a leap from the premise of a just war in theory to a conclusion that the wars we fight are just. The moral convention forms a symbiosis of ethics and application. The convention allows us to be fooled into thinking of rules as reality. All who are touched by war see some wreckage left from this betrayal. They glimpse the face of war that wears the mask of rules; even when it keeps the mask on, war will have its way. What's wrong wears a mask of "what's right"; the untrustworthiness of war depends first on my trust in the ethics of war. Military personnel are not the only people who put trust in an ethics of war; so does the American public. Even if civilians condemn this ongoing war on moral ground, they still support it through their tax dollars, elected officials, and institutions of government.

What has gone awry in the global war on terror is at the heart of just war theory: if the principles of just war are to function at all, soldiers on both sides of a conflict should be treated as "moral equals."[51] As I have noted in chapter 2, the pretenses of a unique American sovereignty and moral superiority are premises that rule out the possibility of our enemies in the global war on terror ever being treated as "moral equals." The lives of others are already devalued, dehumanized. We go to war putting our trust in a convention of rightness, but in war there is a "visceral experience of policy, as well as cultural assumptions, that are put into effect corporately on the ground through the bodies of soldiers and others."[52] The convention, the language of goodness, justice, and freedom, is revealed to us as wrong through what we *live* in war. What is enacted is a "kind of hatred"; the other has been labeled evil by our highest political authorities, and our language of justice in practice is to "do evil to the evil."[53]

Living out the policy and the rhetoric of Bush's "conflict between good and evil" belongs to those on the lower end of the chain of command. Those who live it are betrayed by the convention—they end up doubly fucked. The convention at home, the convention that is supposed to be something other than war, betrays them when what they are most ashamed of is honored and enshrined: "[. . .] even your mother is so happy and proud because you lined up your sight posts and made people crumple [. . .]"[54]

Goodness, justice, freedom (life)—the principles, ideals, and values used as justification for the global war on terror—are stripped away in the war itself. The moral convention of the war lacks goodness, justice, and freedom and instead operates as domination (anti-life). The language of what ought to be is conflated with what is. Those who embody the language of war on the ground experience what the war really is—that which ought not be; they are betrayed by the convention. This is the negative revelation of war—a stripping away of the moral convention of anti-life. One is left with the desire for what ought to be, which is glimpsed through negation and rejection of that which should not be. What ought to be is not secure, absolute, rigid, and static. It is fragile and flickering. One cannot grasp it in war; one can only see clearly what it is not. The convention of the global war on terror presents an antithesis to life, set up as reality, enshrined as what is good. Life is denied in the convention. The absence of life in the moral convention of the global war on terror comprises the "moral" component of moral injury.

NOTES

1. Tim O'Brien, *The Things They Carried* (Boston, MA: Mariner Books, 2009), 77.

2. Simone Weil, "The Love of God and Affliction," in *Waiting for God* (New York: Harper Perennial, 2001), 67–82. See especially p. 75: "God can never be perfectly present to us here below on account of our flesh. But [God] can be almost perfectly absent from us in extreme affliction."

3. Origen, *On First Principles*, trans. G. W. Butterworth (Notre Dame, IN: Christian Classics, 2013), 125.

4. Walzer's exposition of the theory hinges on this moral equality: "the moral status of individual soldiers on both sides is very much the same: they are led to fight by their loyalty to their own states and by their lawful obedience. They are most likely to believe that their wars are just, and while the basis of that belief is not necessarily

rational inquiry but, more often, a kind of unquestioning acceptance of official propaganda, nevertheless they are not criminals; they face one another as moral equals." See Walzer, *Just and Unjust Wars: A Moral Argument with Historical Illustrations*, 5th edition (New York: Basic Books, 2015), 34–41, 127.

5. O'Brien, *The Things They Carried*, 77.

6. Michael Yandell, "Do Not Torment Me: The Morally Injured Gerasene Demoniac," in *Moral Injury: A Guidebook for Understanding and Engagement*, ed. Brad Kelle (New York: Lexington Books, 2020), 72.

7. Martha C. Nussbaum, "Finely Aware and Richly Responsible: Literature and the Moral Imagination," in *Love's Knowledge: Essays on Philosophy and Literature* (New York: Oxford University Press, 1990), 148–67, 162.

8. Kevin Powers, *The Yellow Birds: A Novel* (New York: Little, Brown and Company, 2012), 145.

9. Brian Stiltner, *Toward Thriving Communities: Virtue Ethics as Social Ethics* (Winona, MN: Anselm Academic, 2016), 20.

10. Ibid., 20–21.

11. George W. Bush, "Commencement Address at the United States Military Academy in West Point, New York," *Weekly Compilation of Presidential Documents* 38, no. 2 (June 10, 2002): 944–48.

12. Shay, Jonathan, *Achilles in Vietnam: Combat Trauma and the Undoing of Character* (New York: Scribner, 1994), 3.

13. Ibid., 5.

14. Ibid., 12.

15. Shay, Jonathan, *Odysseus in America: Combat Trauma and the Trials of Homecoming* (New York: Scribner, 2002), 240.

16. Shay, *Achilles in Vietnam*, 5–6.

17. Ibid., 20.

18. Brett T. Litz, Nathan Stein, Eileen Delaney, Leslie Lebowitz, William P. Nash, Caroline Silva, Shira Maguen, "Moral Injury and Moral Repair in War Veterans: A Preliminary Model and Intervention Strategy," *Clinical Psychology Review* 29, no. 8 (December 2009): 695–706, 697.

19. Ibid., 699.

20. Jonathan Shay, "Moral Injury," *Psychoanalytic Psychology* 31, no. 2 (2014): 182–91, 184.

21. For a practical theological examination of multiple moralities in play, see Zachary Moon, *Warriors Between Worlds: Moral Injury and Identities in Crisis* (New York: Lexington Books, 2019). Moon uses the term "moral orienting systems" to nuance the moral identity and formation of military personnel—who they were before military service, during, and after.

22. For example, in a recent empirical clinical study regarding moral injury outcomes, "killing within the rules of engagement" is identified as one potentially morally injurious event on a questionnaire used with patients: Julie D. Yeterian et al., "Defining and Measuring Moral Injury: Rationale, Design, and Preliminary Findings from the Moral Injury Outcome Scale Consortium," *Journal of Traumatic Stress* 32, no. 3 (June 1, 2019): 363–72.

23. See, for example, Jacob K. Farnsworth, "Is and Ought: Descriptive and Prescriptive Cognitions in Military-Related Moral Injury," *Journal of Traumatic Stress* 32, no. 3 (June 1, 2019): 373–81.

24. Warren Kinghorn, "Combat Trauma and Moral Fragmentation: A Theological Account of Moral Injury," *Journal of the Society of Christian Ethics* 32, no. 2 (2012): 57–74, 67.

25. For accounts of veterans attempting to name a deeper reality, see also Rita Nakashima Brock and Gabriella Lettini, *Soul Repair: Recovering from Moral Injury after War* (Boston, MA: Beacon Press, 2012).

26. Powers, *The Yellow Birds*, 145.

27. Tyler Boudreau, "The Morally Injured," *Massachusetts Review* 52, no. 3/4 (2011): 746–54, 750.

28. Ibid., 751.

29. Joseph Wiinikka-Lydon, "Moral Injury as Inherent Political Critique: The Prophetic Possibilities of a New Term," *Political Theology* 18, no. 3 (May 2017): 219–32, 228.

30. Ibid., 228.

31. For an explicitly theological account of the sin of violence as a distorted good enshrined as value, see Brian S. Powers, *Full Darkness: Original Sin, Moral Injury, and Wartime Violence* (Grand Rapids, MI: William. B. Eerdmans Publishing Company, 2019).

32. Shay, *Achilles in Vietnam*.

33. Martha C. Nussbaum, *The Fragility of Goodness: Luck and Ethics in Greek Tragedy and Philosophy*, Revised edition (New York: Cambridge University Press, 2001), 397–421. Jonathan Shay notes: "Nussbaum's excellent discussion centers on *nomos*, a word that largely supplanted *thémis* in this semantic range. The word *nomos*, which was much used by the Athenian tragic poets, such as Sophocles, is not found in Homer" (*Achilles in Vietnam*, 211).

34. Ibid., 399, 409.

35. Ibid., 400.

36. Ibid.

37. Ibid., 406–407.

38. Ibid., 408.

39. Ibid.

40. Ibid., 413.

41. Michael Walzer, *Just and Unjust Wars: A Moral Argument with Historical Illustrations*, 5th edition (New York: Basic Books, 2015), 337.

42. Ibid., 20.

43. Ibid., 133.

44. Ibid., 138, 152.

45. Ibid., 45.

46. Ibid., 156.

47. Powers, *The Yellow Birds*, 4.

48. Robert E. Meagher, *Killing from the Inside Out: Moral Injury and Just War* (Eugene, OR: Cascade Books, 2014), 129.

49. Ibid., 131–32.
50. Walzer, *Just and Unjust Wars*, 334.
51. Ibid., 34–41, 127.
52. Wiinikka-Lydon, "Moral Injury as Inherent Political Critique," 228.
53. Origen, *On First Principles*, 125.
54. Powers, *The Yellow Birds*, 145.

Chapter 4

Moral Injury as Negative Revelation, Part II

"Injury"—Loss of Meaning

Moral injury is a revelation: "The world is not what I thought it was; I am not who I thought I was"; or, "moral injury is despair of the world and oneself."[1] In chapter 3, I described a moral convention that betrays human beings (the world). The moral convention of the global war on terror enshrines anti-life as life, celebrating the wrongness of domination and death as what's right. The world, described in terms of goodness, justice, and freedom, is revealed as the inverse of these ideals, betraying those who live out the foreign policy of the United States in confrontations with its declared enemies. One despairs of the world as the world betrays individuals.

The "injury" component of moral injury is about despairing of oneself. If the moral convention I dedicate my life to upholding is not what I thought it was, then who am I? The reasons people commit their lives to military service are varied and nuanced. Many of us, to some degree, wanted to strive for some semblance of justice in the world after 9/11/2001. In our striving, we found our lives "harnessed to wars that ran far past the pursuit of justice and ultimately did not succeed."[2] One despairs of oneself as one betrays the world.

The injury runs deeper than the experience of failure after trying one's best. One begins to suspect that the war itself succeeds; the failure is in our understanding of it. The global war on terror is not a temporary measure; it is a framework, a system of meaning that attempts to exhaustively explain and define human life. The war continues, coming of age; soon it will be older than some service members being sent to fight it. The war is a system that explains everything in terms of civility and terror, good and evil, friend and enemy. Some of us continue to try and claw our way out of this system. The war explains us away as warriors, victims, heroes, villains, wounded, dead, and displaced. The war succeeds in defining us all as more or less than we are. Drowned in explanation and definition, where does one go for air?

I use the word injury in the sense of a "loss sustained."[3] Chapter 3 describes layers of negative revelation. First, the false sense of goodness that hides the deeper layer of domination (anti-life) in the moral convention of war; second, the glimpse past anti-life itself—the aching for what could be. As the layers of the moral convention's betrayal of persons are peeled back, layers of the person are also peeled back. In a sense, we lose what we never had, and long for it. I thought I was a defender and protector of life; I found myself in the service of anti-life—diminishing my own life and the lives of others.

And yet.

The loss sustained is the loss of an illusion—the breach of a false reality.

Even the first layer—to be a defender and protector of life—is part of war's explanation of life, part of its gaze, that puts me in conflict with the "enemy" always in the polar opposite role, but understood and comprehended only in relation to me and what/who I am as a soldier.

I lost the illusion that I was in the service of goodness and justice, and I became convinced that I was not good, that I was unjust, that I was condemned.

And yet.

This is also illusion. How so? Stripped bare, I want to do the good. I want life.

Life resists anti-life; life overflows the explanations and definitions of war. What happens to the person betrayed by moral convention? What loss does one sustain? "Doubly fucked"[4] as Kevin Powers puts it—betrayer and betrayed—to speak of my betrayal of the good in war is nonsense when the convention perpetuating the war is still celebrated as the good. Just as "what's right" seemed to make sense in war, so did *my life*. In war, one sustains a loss of a world that makes moral sense;[5] in losing that world, one loses a sense of who one is. *I don't know who I am.* Paul Tillich reminds, however: "The act of accepting meaninglessness is itself a meaningful act."[6]

Chapter 3 focused on the negative revelation of the world—a moral convention hiding anti-life. This chapter focuses on the negative revelation of the self. In this chapter, I am attempting to go all the way down. Moral injury is a negative revelation—a recognition of anti-life illusions that have posed as life. Moral injury is despair of the world and the self, compromised and assaulted by anti-life. Moral injury, taken all the way down, is accepting the meaninglessness of these anti-life constructs. This experience of acceptance is itself meaningful.

THE INTELLIGIBLE SELF

In this section, I borrow from the work of Alasdair MacIntyre to present a concept of the human "self" that is intelligible. It is precisely this sort of intelligible self that I am claiming is lost in the experience of moral injury; moreover, the intelligible self is revealed to have never been. In *After Virtue*, MacIntyre's primary purpose is to salvage an account of the virtues that is true to the Western tradition dating back to Aristotle while also providing course corrections for that tradition in order to make it comprehensible to the modern era. Whether MacIntyre succeeds remains a topic of copious debate among philosophers and ethicists. My purpose is not to attack MacIntyre or to debate the fine points of his argument. I draw on him because his account of self-hood is compelling, not least because of its emphasis on relationship and community. It is perhaps alluring to those of us at home in the Western tradition. However, his framework leaves little space for experiences of trauma, moral injury, and world-rending.

MacIntyre highlights several conflicting theories of virtues in the Western tradition, focusing on Homer, Aristotle, the New Testament, Ben Franklin, and Jane Austen. In constructing his own account of virtues, MacIntyre notes a commonality in these conflicting theories: the concept of a virtue "always requires for its application the acceptance for some prior account of certain features of social and moral life in terms of which it has to be defined and explained."[7] Virtues are secondary to "social roles" for Homer, to "the good life [. . .] as *telos* of human action" for Aristotle, and to "utility" for Franklin.[8] These background features of social and moral life render the virtues intelligible in the work of Homer, Aristotle, and Franklin. MacIntyre's own background for his theory of virtue depends on three conceptual stages: "practices, [. . .] the narrative order of a single human life, [. . .] and what constitutes a moral tradition."[9]

MacIntyre's "narrative order of a single human life" is central to my claims in this chapter about the loss of self endured in moral injury, but first his concept of "practices" needs elaboration. MacIntyre defines a "practice" as

> any coherent and complex form of socially established cooperative human activity through which goods internal to that form of activity are realized in the course of trying to achieve those standards of excellence which are appropriate to, and partially definitive of, that form of activity, with the result that human powers to achieve excellence, and human conceptions of the ends and goods involved, are systematically extended.[10]

One clear example of a practice that MacIntyre provides to clarify this lengthy definition is playing chess. Some "internal goods" of chess-playing include "analytical skill, strategic imagination and competitive intensity."[11] One gains the internal goods appropriate to chess by engaging in the practice of chess-playing. Practices also often come with external goods, but external goods are not linked necessarily with virtue. In MacIntyre's example, one might teach a child to play chess by offering a reward of candy (external good) for time spent practicing chess. If a child wants candy, she might cheat at chess to get it, thus circumventing gaining the goods internal to chess-playing. The hope is that the child, over time, will value the goods internal to chess over the external goods, engaging in the practice of chess in order to excel at chess rather than to receive candy. What is important is that practices, which include a wide range such as "arts, sciences, politics [and so on]" come with a history and a community of practitioners.

The link between practices and virtues for MacIntyre is the relationship among practitioners. A virtue, for MacIntyre, becomes "an acquired human quality the possession and exercise of which tends to enable us to achieve those goods which are internal to practices and the lack of which effectively prevents us from achieving any such goods."[12] Virtues are acquired, and the goods internal to practices are achieved, "by subordinating ourselves within the practice in our relationship to other practitioners."[13] We have to accept some measure of "justice, courage and honesty" in order to receive criticism, learn from those who already excel at a practice, and strive for excellence and the goods internal to a practice. Cheating only gets us candy, not virtue.[14] Virtue, here, requires just, courageous, and honest subordination.

Practicing Life as a Soldier

Any person with a relationship to the U.S. military is familiar with the language of subordination. Upon enlistment to military service, a person will seal her commitment by pledging an oath before the American flag in the presence of others:

> I, _____, do solemnly swear (or affirm) that I will support and defend the Constitution of the United States against all enemies, foreign and domestic; that I will bear true faith and allegiance to the same; and that I will obey the orders of the President of the United States and the orders of the officers appointed over me, according to regulations and the Uniform Code of Military Justice. So help me God.[15]

In swearing to obey orders, there is an inherent "willingness to trust the judgments of those whose achievement in the practice give them an authority to judge which presupposes fairness and truthfulness in the judgments, and from time to time the taking of self-endangering and even achievement-endangering risks."[16] That is to say, to defend the Constitution against enemies is a specific kind of practice, one that requires my subordination to its institutional form in order to achieve the internal goods of that practice.

Focusing on the U.S. Army as one of the institutional branches of the military, joining the Army is to enter into relationship with practitioners of soldiering. I subordinate myself to become a good soldier, to gain the qualities necessary to achieve the goods internal to the practice of soldiering. In the initial stages of basic training, I may perform tasks simply to receive the "candy" that is avoiding mass punishment from drill instructors. Day by day, I may begin to help other soldiers because I begin to understand that being a soldier is being part of a team, a unit. By the time I arrive at a duty station, hopefully I no longer need the threat of the ever-present drill instructor as motivation; I have accepted the standards of excellence in soldiering as my own.

The standards of excellence and the virtues required for achieving the internal goods of soldering are codified in texts and recited aloud in training environments and in front of promotion boards. MacIntyre suggests that there are two kinds of internal goods in practices. The first is the "excellence of the products"; for example, in painting, the excellence of a painting itself. The second kind of internal good is "the good of a certain kind of life," what one discovers "within the pursuit of excellence"; for example, "life *as a painter.*"[17] In the U.S. Army, the "Soldier's Creed" defines *life as a soldier*:

I am an American Soldier.
I am a warrior and a member of a team.
I serve the people of the United States, and live the Army Values.
I will always place the mission first.
I will never accept defeat.
I will never quit.
I will never leave a fallen comrade.
I am disciplined, physically and mentally tough, trained and proficient in my warrior tasks and drills.
I always maintain my arms, my equipment and myself.
I am an expert and I am a professional.
I stand ready to deploy, engage, and destroy, the enemies of the United States of America in close combat.
I am a guardian of freedom and the American way of life.
I am an American Soldier.[18]

One takes on *life as a soldier* by acting out the statements in this Creed. The practice becomes *who one is*. The "Army Values" referenced in the third line are "loyalty, duty, respect, selfless service, honor, integrity, and personal courage" (LDRSHIP).[19] The drill instructor uses her methods of mass punishment to mold her soldiers into "warriors and members of a team." The soldier subordinates herself to become a good soldier, trusting in some measure her superiors who have already proven themselves good soldiers, exhibiting the "LDRSHIP" virtues of the practice.

MacIntyre stresses that "any account of the virtues in terms of practices [can] only be a partial and first account."[20] For a fuller account of the virtues, MacIntyre raises the Aristotelian concern for *telos*, the overriding question, "what is the good life?" Without a concept of *telos* or ultimate end toward which life is oriented, an account of the virtues based solely on practices is limited in three ways. First, arbitrariness: there are a multiplicity of goods and multiple allegiances which may come into conflict. Second, without some overriding *telos*, there can be no ordering and evaluating of goods internal to a practice. MacIntyre provides the example of patience, that is, patience *for what*? One may find reason to exercise patience in a specific practice, but without a *telos* there is no reason for exercising patience as a virtue beyond that practice. Third, MacIntyre names "one virtue recognized by the tradition which cannot be specified at all except with reference to the wholeness of a human life—the virtue of integrity or constancy."[21]

The concern for *telos* brings us to MacIntyre's second and third stages of conceptualizing virtue, after the first of practices: "the narrative order of a single human life, [. . .] and what constitutes a moral tradition."[22] MacIntyre claims: "The unity of a human life is the unity of a narrative quest"; moreover, it is a quest for "the good."[23] The "good" here is the concept of *telos*, and what it means to quest for the good for a particular person depends on the unity of her life as narrative. The narrative order of a single human life is "a concept of self whose unity resides in the unity of a narrative which links birth to life to death as narrative beginning to middle to end."[24] The necessary components for a unity of narrative, for understanding the individual "self" and what it is doing, are "behaviors, intentions, and settings": "We cannot [. . .] characterize behavior independently of intentions, and we cannot characterize intentions independently of the settings which make those intentions intelligible both to agents themselves and to others."[25] As one attends to a narrative of a human life, one must also attend to the history of settings, "within which the histories of individual agents not only are, but have to be, situated, just because without the setting and its changes through time the history of the individual agent and his [sic] changes through time will be unintelligible."[26]

Intelligibility is key for MacIntyre. We render actions and selves intelligible by finding their place in a narrative, understanding the setting, behaviors, and intentions that contextualize the narrative, in order to "understand our own lives in terms of the narratives that we live out."[27] We understand our actions only by asking the question, "Of what story or stories do I find myself a part?"[28] This leads MacIntyre to the concept of "strict identity": "I am forever whatever I have been at any time for others—and I may at any time be called upon to answer for it—no matter how changed I may be now. . . . The self inhabits a character whose unity is given as the unity of a character."[29]

Strict identity gets at the heart of how one can feel wrong about what was "right" in war. Some of us who live life as veterans now have changed much since our experiences of war. However, we are never *not* the people who fought. War, in our narratives, spanned a unit of time that can be measured, but if we accept the concept of "strict identity," then we are *now* what we were *then*, no matter how much we would like it to be otherwise. Of course, we are also more than what we were. We have been different at different times for different people, and people have been different for us. This is the two-fold requirement of a narrative concept of selfhood, according to MacIntyre: "I am what I may justifiably be taken by others to be in the course of living out a story that runs from my birth to my death [. . . but] I am not only accountable, I am one who can always ask others for an account. . . . I am part of their story, as they are part of mine."[30] For MacIntyre, this capacity to provide and ask for accounts is what makes selves and actions intelligible.

MacIntyre's third stage of the development of virtue is the concept of a moral tradition. His understanding of moral tradition is more complex than the moral convention that received my criticism in chapter 3. MacIntyre offers a complicated and textured analysis of how virtue is related to a larger social world. Human beings do not engage in practices and pursue quests for the good in isolation: "the story of my life is always embedded in the story of those communities from which I derive my identity."[31] This communal/social quality is key to MacIntyre's sense of the individual and her identity. The self is "not detachable from its social and historical roles and statuses."[32] The Soldier's Creed provides a clear example of at least two communities from which a soldier derives her identity: other soldiers and citizens of the United States. "I am a warrior and a member of a team. I serve the people of the United States, and I live the Army values." Soldiers and service members can endure great hardship while pursuing the good, and they can maintain an intelligible sense of self while withstanding substantial loss. That is to say, I can understand the story of my life as a soldier as I enact the virtues of loyalty, duty, respect, selfless service, honor, integrity, and personal courage in defense of the Constitution and in service to the people of the United States. The life story makes sense; it is intelligible, even in violent conflict in which one may be remorseful for the supposed necessity of violent action. It makes sense so long as the *telos* holds, the pursuit of the good. There are past wars that the reader, perhaps, may interpret as stories in which the *telos* held—perhaps the narrative of the Nazis' defeat in World War II. *The story of the global war on terror is not such a story.*

MacIntyre's overreliance on intelligibility does not leave enough room, in my view, for the kind of social critique demanded by the reality of the global war on terror. I am not arguing that his concept of moral tradition is itself an anti-life framework of morality. Rather, I am claiming that anti-life has become moral tradition in twenty-first-century warfare. The language of "supporting the troops" and "God bless America" tells a story about a community in which a soldier's identity is formed. This story, woefully incomplete, eclipses the revelation military personnel often experience in living out the global war. Because this false narrative is so thickly intertwined with "what's right" in the broad social and moral fabric of the United States, there is little room for the very soldiers who are supposedly living out the virtues derived from their communities to critique what has gone horrifically wrong.

MacIntyre suggests, "When someone claims—as do some of those who attempt or commit suicide—that his or her life is meaningless, he or she is often and perhaps characteristically complaining that the narrative of their life has become unintelligible to them, that it lacks any point, any movement towards a climax or a *telos*."[33] This may be true, but it is not all of the truth. There is a chasm between freedom and domination. The global war on terror is not intelligible as a story of liberation and life. It is intelligible only as a story of domination. We can speak here of *meaningful lives* embedded and oriented toward a *meaningless telos*. That is, when I see the narrative of my life as a soldier, which I understand as a pursuit of the good, oriented toward the consummation of domination; my loyalty, my duty, my respect, my selfless service, my honor, my integrity, my personal courage—they are rendered meaningless. The story in which I find myself a part—the story of ongoing global war in the twenty-first century—is revealed as a story of anti-life, standing firm as a "moral" tradition with a long history.[34]

"THE ENTRY OF A SURD": DISINTEGRATION OF THE INTELLIGIBLE SELF

"You're going to see a good man disintegrate before your eyes," said a friend of one battalion commander heading to Iraq as part of the "surge."[35] In this section, I draw on brief narrative accounts from military personnel to demonstrate the *disintegration* of MacIntyre's narrative unity of a human life. According to MacIntyre, we make sense of ourselves by asking, "Of what story or stories do I find myself a part?"[36] The story of the global war on terror comes with its own anti-life intelligibility, as recounted in chapters 2 and 3. Anti-life makes nonsense out of individual quests for the good, the quests of individuals who find their lives harnessed to and embedded in the story of the war.

The disintegration of self is not unique to the experience of war. Philosopher Susan Brison, while not in direct dialogue with MacIntyre, illuminates the vast space of trauma for which MacIntyre's narrative unity of life can provide no intelligible account. In *Aftermath: Violence and the Remaking of a Self*, Brison examines her life as a survivor of sexual assault, demonstrating the disruption of narrative and of self. Out of respect for her story, I quote her own words at length:

> On July 4, 1990, at 10:30 in the morning, I went for a walk along a peaceful-looking country road in a village outside Grenoble, France. It was a gorgeous day, and I didn't envy my husband, Tom, who had to stay inside and work on a manuscript with a French colleague of his. I sang to myself as I set out, stopping to pet a goat and pick a few wild strawberries along the way. About an hour and a half later, I was lying face down in a muddy creek bed at the bottom of a dark ravine, struggling to stay alive. I had been grabbed from behind, pulled into the bushes, beaten, and sexually assaulted.[37]

Brison describes what happened to her and what happens to other victims of violence as a "disintegration of the self" that "challenges our notions of personal identity over time."[38] For Brison, trauma "introduces a 'surd'—a nonsensical entry—into the series of events in one's life, making it seem impossible to carry on with the series."[39] One is supposed to be able to take a jog on a gorgeous day in the morning without being raped and left for dead. So long as one's life is constituted by a series of jogs in the morning that do not end in violent trauma, the series makes sense. The life makes sense. The world offers a trustworthy pattern in which a jog is not threatening. One has a satisfactory answer to the question: "Of what story or stories do I find myself a part?" The entry of the "surd," Brison's horrific account of rape in broad daylight, reveals the old intelligible, trustworthy pattern as inherently *untrustworthy*—as nonsense.

Much of Brison's book is her story of her own recovery, and how that recovery relates to what she knew—or thought she knew—about the "self" and the world from her own philosophical training and work. Brison states, "Recovery no longer seems to consist of picking up the pieces of a shattered self (or fractured narrative). It's facing the fact that there never was a coherent self (or story) there to begin with."[40] Brison also maintains that we are socially constructed, "in large part through our group-based narratives, [therefore] the self is not a single, unified, coherent entity."[41] It is the energy of relationality from which narratives flow, not isolated individuals. Brison argues: "Even those who are able to acknowledge the existence of violence try to protect themselves from the realization that the world in which it occurs is their world and so they find it hard to identify with the victim."[42] To protect oneself is to hold only to an *individual* story, for example, "the story of my life does not contain violence; thus, your story of violence is not a story taking place in my world." Brison is saying that *our* story, *our* world, is a violent world. There is not another world or another story in which violence is absent. To believe otherwise is to trust in a moral convention that is inherently false and untrustworthy.

I do not wish to twist Brison's story into anything other than her story. However, the entry of the "surd" (the moment where a pattern, a series, and world that make sense, are revealed as nonsense) applies directly to the experience of war. In Brison's case, violence was the surd in an otherwise sensical series of jogs in the morning.

In war, the series is violence. Violence is expected. Meaning is ascribed to the violence; for instance, the Soldier's Creed: "I stand ready to deploy, engage, and destroy, the enemies of the United States of America in close combat. I am a guardian of freedom and the American way of life." Meaning is ascribed to the violence by politicians and planners of war. However, in the daily lived experience of people fighting the global war on terror in Iraq, the series of violence is revealed as absurd—only disrupted by occasional glimpses of goodness and decency, frustratingly fragile and fleeting. Recalling MacIntyre, to get the sense of a narrative unity of a human life, one must also attend to behaviors, intentions, and settings. One may intend to do the good even when one acts violently, to "guard freedom," but with the global war on terror, the whole *setting is fucked*. Women and men attempting to do the good find themselves in a setting that has nothing to do with freedom. On the one hand, they discover that the war is not what it seemed when sold to the American public. On the other hand, they see a world soaked in violence and trauma—a world the reality of which belies the very notion of intelligible narratives and intelligible selves. The narrative logic of defense and freedom and war and sacrifice—the story that keeps the machinery of war operating smoothly in the United States—is a logic that eclipses and obscures the war itself from those who do not see it first-hand. Those who do see it begin to question all such anti-life logics.

Fragments of Revelation

In perhaps Donald Rumsfeld's most profound utterance of his career, as his resignation and replacement was announced, he described the global war on terror to President Bush as "this little understood, unfamiliar war, the first war of the 21st century—it is not well-known, it was not well-understood, it is complex for people to comprehend."[43]

The war is impossible to understand if one attempts to view it as if one is outside of it. The world at war is the world we live in—it is not separated from us. The story of all our lives is embedded in the violence of war. Thus, the war is not something which can be comprehended and understood. The war itself is a system, a framework of comprehension, a setting that attempts to determine what human beings are. What follows are fragments, real-life accounts that pierce and begin to tear away the veil of global war's comprehension of human beings.

Decency and Hatred

It was important to Major Brent Cummings of the 2-16 Infantry Battalion, deployed to Iraq in 2007, to act with decency.[44] Cummings knew that there was "goodness in the country" [of Iraq]: "'I would hope someone would do the same for my body. And for any human being. Otherwise we're not human,' he said."[45] The factory was destroyed by unidentified masked men soon after Cummings and his soldiers visited it. Upon hearing the news, Cummings remarked "I hate this place." About a month later, following the fourth death in his battalion, Cummings wrote, "I hate this place [. . .] the way it smells [. . .] the way it looks. [. . .] I hate the way these people don't care about freedom, I hate that human beings want to kill each other over nothing."[46] A year later, having suffered numerous losses and witnessing the ruin of the sewer system the battalion had worked to bring to the area of Rustamiyah, Cummings said, "Stupid people. I hate 'em. Stupid fucking scumbags."[47]

Major Cummings, as his story is told in *The Good Soldiers*, is by no means a hateful person. He wanted "Bob" to have a proper burial. He risked bending rules so that the young daughter of an interpreter could receive life-saving medical care on an American forward operating base.[48] He seems to embody Tim O'Brien's words, "In the midst of evil you want to be a good man. You want decency."[49] Of what story or stories is Major Cummings a part? Why the articulation of hatred—for the place, for the people? Cummings's story is his own, but I suggest that "the midst of evil" here, to borrow from O'Brien, is not about Iraq and its people. It is about an invaded and occupied Iraq, subjected to forces of domination. Cummings, "Bob," the interpreter's daughter, the destroyed sewer system—these narratives are part of a larger narrative: the global war. *The setting is fucked.*

What Is Seen and Known

On May 15, 2007, President Bush went to the National Naval Medical Center in Bethesda, Maryland, and visited Sergeant Michael Emory—a man who had been shot in the head in Iraq and was now "diapered, who could barely move, who had a ventilator tube inserted into his throat, who was looking in panic at his wife who was armored in a mask and gown and gloves."[50] After President Bush thanked her for her husband's service, Maria Emory thanked him for coming, though she wished to say:

[H]e didn't understand what we are going through because he *doesn't* know how it feels. And that I didn't agree with what was going on in the war. [. . .] I mean, when I saw him, I was so angry I started crying, and he saw me and came to me and gave me a hug and said, "Everything's going to be okay." That was why he came over to her, she said, because he misunderstood the reason for her tears. He'd had no idea they were because of anger, and he'd had no idea they were because of him. And nothing was okay, she said, so he was wrong about that too.[51]

Months later, when LTC Kauzlarich (Battalion commander for the 2-16 Infantry, Michael Emory's unit) was in the United States on a short leave from deployment, he also paid Michael Emory and other wounded soldiers of the 2-16 a visit at Brooke Army Medical Center in San Antonio. He left the hospital saying, "These guys got me all fucking motivated."[52] What he did not know is what Maria Emory did not tell him, that which she knew about her husband:

She wondered: Should she tell him what *she* knew? How depressed her husband was? That one day he had tipped himself over onto a hard tile floor, telling her when she found him that he'd wanted to hit his head and die? That another day he had begged her to get him a knife? That another day he had asked for a pen so he could push it into his neck? That another day, instead of asking for a knife or a pen, he'd tried to bite through his wrists?[53]

What Maria knows is part of a hidden knowledge of war, an "unknown known" that usually remains obscured at the margins of war discourse—the disintegration of selves and narratives. The hidden knowledge, unknown by many citizens but known by Maria, is how quickly and completely lives are swept up and emptied into the narrative of war. David Finkel rightly describes the war in Iraq as a different war than the one in the United States. In the United States "the news was all macro rather than micro"; politicians and pundits on mainstream news programs would "do some screaming [. . .] to listen to them was to listen to people who knew everything. They knew why the surge was working. They knew why the surge wasn't working. They not only screamed, they screamed with certainty."[54] In the United States, the war is a political narrative, a "point of discussion";[55] it pays no mind to concrete life, instead comprehending life through a lens of anti-life. The only way to scream with certainty over war as a point of discussion is to disregard life itself and to pretend that one is living in a different world, a world in which violence is not part of one's life. The failures and successes of war are debated ad nauseum by people maintaining an artificial distance from the war—as if they can speak of it objectively having never reckoned with its reality—while the hidden life, the seen but unknown, begs his spouse for a knife.

"This War is Complete Bullshit . . ."[56]

"Of what story or stories do I find myself a part?"[57] The answer to this question provides the means to make sense of oneself or to make oneself intelligible, according to MacIntyre—how one sees one's life oriented to a *telos*, an end, the pursuit of the good. When one pursues justice in the midst of the global war on terror, justice remains elusive; the *telos* crumbles, and so does one's sense of oneself. As part of the study *Operation Recovery*, when asked "What are the major causes of soldier trauma?", one soldier responded:

> I think the major cause of the soldier's trauma is there's nothing to be proud of. That's my personal belief. I don't even think that everybody understands that that's what it is. But I think, deep down, everyone knows that there is no reason for the Iraq War. I think, deep down there, everybody knows that. [. . .] I think it's like a light switch. If one day you realize, "Shit. Everything I went to, everything I did, was bullshit. It didn't matter," then that changes all your experiences.[58]

Ryan Holleran responded:

> Primarily, being deployed in a fucking place where you're forced to kill people, you don't know why, and you're forced to fucking watch your buddies die, and you don't know why. Even to the mentality of the day-to-day, you're living in a world who's [sic] foundation is violence and domination. And . . . I don't think those are very natural ways to live.[59]

Telling the story of Specialist Robert Soto's 2010 deployment to Afghanistan, C. J. Chivers describes him as "the type of grunt that long wars will make: the young enlisted soldier, sick of bullshit, who fought just to keep his friends alive."[60] In the midst of absurd circumstances, Soto sees the global war on terror with remarkable clarity as he thinks to himself: "We're here because we're here. We're here because another unit came here and set up, and we replaced them, and no one knows what else to do."[61] Soto's thoughts echo those of World War I soldiers fighting in the trenches, singing "We're here / Because / We're Here / Because / We're here / Because we're here."[62]

The war on terror comprises a narrative, a story in which women and men—many of whom desire to act decently and pursue justice—find themselves a part. As Chivers so poignantly puts it, they found our lives "harnessed to wars that ran far past the pursuit of justice and ultimately did not succeed."[63] One finds one's life oriented toward nothing. Shifting aims of WMD, liberation, security, and so on disintegrate into "here because we're here"—a *telos* of poisoned justice and failure. To see this, to come to terms with the war's hidden knowledge, is not merely the entry of a surd into an otherwise meaningful sequence—it is to recognize that the setting of one's life *is* the absurd. One is left in a state of utter meaninglessness.

THE AFFIRMATION OF MEANINGLESSNESS

The theory and tradition of "just war" has long dealt with two primary aspects of war: the justice or injustice of the war itself (*jus ad bellum*), and the just or unjust means by which the war is fought (*jus in bello*).[64] The *jus ad bellum* category is about the cause, the reasons, goals, and ends—or the *telos*—of war. When one affirms that the global war on terror is an unjust war, one can still strive to act justly and with decency as one fights the war—this is the *jus in bello* category. Major Cummings, who wanted to properly bury the body discovered in a septic tank, exemplifies the idea of just means. The category of *jus in bello*, the conduct of the war, is what enables us to become even more morally outraged by the abuses at Abu Ghraib if we were already morally outraged by the invasion and occupation of Iraq. When I say that coming to terms with war's negative revelation leaves one in a state of utter meaninglessness, I do not mean to say that one's pursuit of justice and decency in war ultimately do not matter. Treating a prisoner with dignity and respect, for example, is clearly to be valued over abusing and torturing that prisoner. The meaninglessness that I am emphasizing here is *that the person is a prisoner at all.*

Paul Tillich asserted: "The act of accepting meaninglessness is itself a meaningful act."[65] I argue that the acceptance of meaninglessness is a crucial component to moral injury as I am describing it, moral injury in which one despairs of the world and oneself. Recalling MacIntyre, "the story of my life is always embedded in the story of those communities from which I derive my identity."[66] When one begins to see the war one fights as unjust or meaningless, that sense of injustice and meaninglessness reflects back on the self. If one derives some sense of identity from "life as a soldier," the *telos* of the war matters much to the *telos* of one's life. The story of one's life as soldier is embedded in the story of the global war on terror—the story of the United States, that which one is supposedly defending in war on the world stage. One's life as a soldier is described in oaths and creeds, and one takes on military values such as leadership, duty, respect, selfless service, honor, integrity, and personal courage in order to pursue justice through support and defense of the U.S. Constitution. Going to war is the culmination of this life as a soldier. When the war is recognized as meaningless, when one sees that its *telos* is not justice, then the oaths, the creeds, and the values forming the life of the soldier are rendered unintelligible, bereft of meaning.

The depth of the negative revelation: As a soldier I wanted *justice*, but the story of my life as a soldier has been embedded in a story of *injustice*. One can act justly in war by trying one's best to treat human beings with decency, but meaninglessness is affirmed in the sense that these efforts do not contribute to a *telos* of justice. Nonetheless, one perpetually waits for the good to come. As Rachel, an Iraqi interpreter, put it: "When I began this, it was safe. Everybody loved the Americans. . . . You figure out a way to handle it. For me, it's a lot of crying, thinking the good is coming. Nothing good has come yet."[67] *Jus in bello*, the conduct of the war, weighs on one's life as merely a list of proscriptions (e.g, do not torture, do not kill civilians, and so on). One finds one's actions meaningless in that proscriptions at best mitigate injustices; they do not form a positive *telos*, a pursuit of the good, a bringing about of justice. This is how the affirmation of meaninglessness in the global war on terror is meaningful, as a negative statement such as Tim O'Brien's "aching love for the way the world could be and always should be, but now is not."[68] Following the dictates of the war convention, what is allowed and what is forbidden, does not bring about the actual good and the justice that one longs for.[69]

I want to briefly revisit medical discourse on moral injury to highlight how my conception of moral injury differs. Put briefly, the medical model prioritizes the need for forgiveness and integration, because moral injury in that model is tied to specific acts and events as moral transgressions. I want to shift the focus from forgiveness to justice. Moral injury as a loss sustained, as a despair of oneself and the world, is a recognition of the loss of justice—or that justice was never the end of war and my life as a soldier. The world's justice, in the form of the anti-life convention of war outlined in chapter 3, has been revealed as a kind of hatred, an orientation toward domination and anti-life. The wrongness of war is celebrated as what's right. Moral injury is an affirmation of the meaninglessness of the world's justice.

For Litz et al., the problem presented with moral injury is that an individual attributes the cause of a moral transgression in a way that "is *global* (i.e., not context dependent), *internal* (i.e., seen as a disposition or character flaw), and *stable* (i.e., enduring; the experience of being tainted) [. . .] these beliefs will cause enduring moral emotions such as shame and anxiety due to uncertainty and the expectation of being judged *eventually*."[70] Again, this model is a vital contribution so long as a moral transgression is a specific act or event. The medical model is an intervention that relieves crisis in the lives of individuals, when transgressions cause an individual with moral injury "to view him or herself as immoral, irredeemable, and un-reparable or believe that he or she lives in an immoral world."[71] The medical model seeks to help people out of that deterministic view of self and world:

> If the person accommodates the experience and attributes the event in a specific (i.e., highly context [war]) dependent, not stable (i.e., time-locked), and external (e.g., a result of exigencies and extraordinary demands) way, this reduces conflict and fosters moral repair; successful integration of the moral violation into an intact, although more flexible, functional belief system.[72]

However, when one is reckoning with the injustice of global war, one is reckoning with a meaninglessness that is not contained by context. The war *is* global and is celebrated as "what's right" in the United States even as specific causes and outcomes of the war are critiqued. Moreover, the war is proving to be quite stable, a fixture of the twenty-first century. Lastly, what is at stake here is not that the morally injured person will be judged eventually for her actions; she has *already judged* the war, and by extension her life, practice, and narrative as a soldier, as meaningless.

Integration of this type of moral violation into "an intact, although more flexible, functional belief system," simply will not do. Recalling the work of Joseph Wiinikka-Lydon, I am talking about a "visceral experience of policy," where one sees "deeply and radically into the truth of the present and how one's country is actually affecting others throughout the world."[73] When one sees deeply how one's life as a soldier is actually affecting others, when one sees that one's efforts toward goodness and justice are foiled by the unjust war one's life is harnessed to, one cannot integrate the negative revelation into an intact belief system. The person, and what she knows about the world, is radically changed. She needs a new way of being, a new *life*.

Susan Brison asks herself and her readers what was needed for her recovery from trauma beyond medication; her answer: "A reconceptualization of the world and my place in it."[74] One can hear an echo of *Hecuba* here; Hecuba remade her world and her place in it with pure revenge. Hecuba's way out is not the only way out. Brison writes, "if recovery means being able to incorporate this awful knowledge into my life and carry on, then, yes, I'm recovered." How is this accomplished? For Brison, the incorporation of awful knowledge into her life takes the form of "Pascal's wager," which she interprets and summarizes: "one makes a wager, in which nothing is certain and the odds change daily, and sets about willing to believe that life, for all its unfathomable horror, still holds some undiscovered pleasures."[75] This is how the old world that betrayed is re-conceptualized, how the coherent self that never was is remade into something new. The world and moral convention are untrustworthy; the world is horrific. The world is also a source of mystery and pleasure.

What of the self, the self of which one despairs in moral injury? MacIntyre's narrative unity has been destroyed. Anti-life poisons and usurps the *telos* to which the convention of just war is oriented. Life as a soldier, with its accompanying practices, values, traditions, and the community in which it is formed and embedded, is rendered unintelligible as a pursuit of the good. "Nothing good has come yet," said Rachel, who worked for years with the Americans. And nothing good will come, not from the old story. Despairing of self and world, where does one turn to keep from drowning? Where is the anti-dote for anti-life's poison?

Looking backward, attempting to find meaning in the war, to find justice in domination, to live life through the Army values that shaped one as a soldier, is meaningless. "The act of accepting meaninglessness is itself a meaningful act."[76] Accepting meaninglessness is a low point of despair, but it is already a turn toward something *new*. One despairs, recognizing that the old meaning that made sense of one's self and world rejected life. Rejecting the old story of anti-life is already an affirmation of life.

In this chapter and the one preceding, I have argued that moral injury is a kind of negative revelation, a despair of the world and oneself. I have focused on the convention that betrays individuals and the experience of meaninglessness felt by individuals. The recognition of this betrayal and the affirmation of meaninglessness comprise moral injury. In the next (and final) chapter, I provide a more thorough analysis of negative revelation—how goodness and justice are "revealed" in this betrayal and meaninglessness.

NOTES

1. Michael Yandell, "Do Not Torment Me: The Morally Injured Gerasene Demoniac," in *Moral Injury: A Guidebook for Understanding and Engagement*, ed. Brad Kelle (New York: Lexington Books, 2020).

2. C.J. Chivers, *The Fighters: Americans in Combat in Afghanistan and Iraq* (New York: Simon and Schuster, 2018), xxii.

3. "Injury," Merriam-Webster dictionary, accessed August 3, 2021, https://www.merriam-webster.com/dictionary/injury.

4. Kevin Powers, *The Yellow Birds: A Novel* (New York: Little, Brown and Company, 2012), 145.

5. Michael Yandell, "The War Within," *Christian Century* 132, no. 1 (January 7, 2015): 12–13.

6. Paul Tillich, *The Courage to Be*, 3rd edition (New Haven, CT: Yale University Press, 2014), 162.

7. Alasdair C MacIntyre, *After Virtue: A Study in Moral Theory*, 3rd edition (Notre Dame, IN: University of Notre Dame Press, 2007), 186.

8. Ibid., 186.

94   Chapter 4

9. Ibid., 186–87.
10. Ibid., 187.
11. Ibid., 188.
12. Ibid., 191.
13. Ibid.
14. Ibid.
15. "Oath of Enlistment," in Title 10, Subtitle A, Part II, Chapter 31, Sec. 502. Accessed August 3, 2021, https://www.govinfo.gov/content/pkg/USCODE-2011-title10/pdf/USCODE-2011-title10-subtitleA-partII-chap31-sec502.pdf This oath is taken by all military personnel across all branches of service.
16. MacIntyre, *After Virtue*, 193.
17. Ibid., 180.
18. "The Soldiers Creed," accessed August 3, 2021, https://www.army.mil/values/soldiers.html. In this section, I focus on the U.S. Army and its language. Each branch of the military service has its own creeds and unique identifiers. A "Soldier" is in the Army, for example, while Marine Corps personnel take on the specific title of "Marine." There are "Sailors" in the Navy, "Airmen" in the Air Force, and "Guardsmen" in the Coast Guard. "Soldier" comes naturally to me when I think of the military, because I was enlisted in the Army. The observations I make regarding creeds and values in this section are specific to the Army, but parallels can be drawn to each branch of service. However, the reader would need to adjust the language to fit the branch of service.
19. "The Army Values," accessed August 3, 2021, https://www.army.mil/values/index.html
20. MacIntyre, *After Virtue*, 201.
21. Ibid., 202–203.
22. Ibid., 186–87.
23. Ibid., 219.
24. Ibid., 205.
25. Ibid., 206.
26. Ibid.
27. Ibid., 210–12.
28. Ibid., 216.
29. Ibid., 217.
30. Ibid., 217–18.
31. Ibid., 221.
32. Ibid.
33. Ibid., 217.
34. In fairness to MacIntyre, he acknowledges in taking up the question of an "evil practice" that "courage sometimes sustains injustice, that loyalty has been known to strengthen a murderous aggressor. . . . That the virtues are defined by not in terms of good or right practices, but of practices, does not entail or imply that practices as actually carried through at particular times and places do not stand in need of moral criticism. And the resources for such criticism are not lacking. There is in the first place no inconsistency in appealing to the requirements of a virtue to criticize a

practice" (p. 200). However, when the tradition and the community from which one has derived one's identity has co-opted the very resources of moral critique, to what may one appeal?

35. David Finkel, *The Good Soldiers* (New York: Picador, 2009), 6. This observation was offered by a friend of Lieutenant Colonel Ralph Kauzlarich, as reported by David Finkel in long-form narrative non-fiction, before Kauzlarich led the 2-16 infantry battalion to eastern Iraq as part of the "surge" in 2007 through 2008. Finkel, a journalist, spent "eight months with the 2-16 in Iraq and made additional reporting trips to Fort Riley, in Kansas; Brooke Army Medical Center, in San Antonio, Texas; the National Naval Medical Center, in Bethesda, Maryland; and Walter Reed Army Medical Center, in Washington, D.C." (p. 317).

36. MacIntyre, *After Virtue*, 216.

37. Susan J. Brison, *Aftermath: Violence and the Remaking of a Self* (Princeton, NJ: Princeton University Press, 2002), 2.

38. Brison, *Aftermath*, 4.

39. Ibid., 103.

40. Ibid., 116.

41. Ibid., 95.

42. Ibid., 9.

43. Secretary Donald Rumsfeld. "President Bush Nominates Dr. Robert M. Gates to be Secretary of Defense." *The White House, the Oval Office*, November 8, 2006, accessed August 3, 2021. https://georgewbush-whitehouse.archives.gov/news/releases/2006/11/20061108-4.html

44. This paragraph very briefly summarizes key events from Cumming's deployment, as recounted in David Finkel, *The Good Soldiers* (New York: Picador, 2009).

45. Finkel, *The Good Soldiers*, 54.

46. Ibid., 85.

47. Ibid., 273.

48. Ibid., 168–73.

49. Tim O'Brien, *The Things They Carried* (Boston, MA: Mariner Books, 2009), 77.

50. Finkel, *The Good Soldiers*, 79–81.

51. Ibid., 82.

52. Ibid., 235.

53. Ibid., 234–35.

54. Ibid., 141–42.

55. Ibid., 149.

56. Finkel, *The Good Soldiers*, 233. This quote is from Joshua Atchley, a wounded soldier of the 2-16 Infantry Battalion, who "wore short-sleeve shirts even though his right arm was terribly scarred: 'I want people to know the price of war.' And what he thought of the war: 'It's bullshit. This war is complete bullshit.' And why he wore a fake eye with a cross-hair patter: 'Because I don't like pretending I have an eye.'"

57. MacIntyre, *After Virtue*, 216.

58. Drake Logan and Adele Carpenter, "Operation Recovery: Fort Hood Soldiers and Veterans Testify on the Right to Heal," May, 2014, accessed August 3, 2021,

https://www.ivaw.org/sites/default/files/documents/Ft%20Hood%20Report.pdf, 58. This report was presented as a joint report on behalf of Iraq Veterans Against the War, Civilian Soldier Alliance, and Under the Hood Café. It includes thirty-one testimonies from soldiers and veterans.

59. *Operation Recovery*, 59.
60. Chivers, *The Fighters*, 214.
61. Ibid.
62. "Soldiers' Song," in *The Penguin Book of First World War Poetry*, ed. George Walter (London: Penguin Classics, 2006), 57.
63. Chivers, *The Fighters*, xxii.
64. For an excellent summary of this "dualism," see especially Michael Walzer, *Just and Unjust Wars: A Moral Argument with Historical Illustrations*, 5th edition (New York: Basic Books, 2015), chapters 2 and 3, 21–50.
65. Tillich, *The Courage to Be*, 162.
66. MacIntyre, *After Virtue*, 221.
67. Finkel, *The Good Soldiers*, 177–78. "Rachel," an Iraqi national, served as an interpreter for the 2-16 infantry battalion during their fifteen-month deployment to Iraq from 2007 to 2008. She had been an interpreter since 2002, and "by her own count, she had been in forty explosions [. . .] burned, knocked out, could no longer hear clearly out of her right ear, and was having trouble seeing out of her left eye" (p. 177).
68. O'Brien, *The Things They Carried*, 77.
69. See Dietrich Bonhoeffer, *Ethics*, ed. Clifford J. Green, trans. Reinhard Krauss, Charles C. West, and Douglas W. Stott, *Dietrich Bonhoeffer Works*, Vol. 6 (Minneapolis, MN: Fortress Press, 2005), 307: "Conscience divides life into permitted and prohibited. There is no commandment. Conscience identifies what is allowed with what is good."
70. Brett T. Litz et al., "Moral Injury and Moral Repair in War Veterans: A Preliminary Model and Intervention Strategy," *Posttraumatic Stress Disorder and the Wars in Afghanistan and Iraq* 29, no. 8 (December 2009): 695–706. doi: 10.1016/j.cpr.2009.07.003, 700.
71. Ibid., 698.
72. Ibid., 701.
73. Joseph Wiinikka-Lydon, "Moral Injury as Inherent Political Critique: The Prophetic Possibilities of a New Term," *Political Theology* 18, no. 3 (May 2017): 219–32, 228.
74. Brison, *Aftermath*, 78.
75. Ibid., 66.
76. Tillich, *The Courage to Be*, 162.

Chapter 5

Negative Revelation and Turning to Life

I have spent some time alluding to a kind of negative revelation in the experience of war, in which previous meanings of goodness and justice fall away and something is revealed of goodness and justice through their absence. I have claimed that the logic of the war is a logic of anti-life, diminishing and defining humanity by the abstract language of the war (e.g., soldier, insurgent, terrorist, patriot). Recalling chapter 1, the language of war is a moral deception—a "morality that dupes," rendering real human beings into superhumans and subhumans through "idolization and contempt."[1] I have argued that the planning and execution of the invasion and occupation of Iraq is a concrete example of anti-life in our time. I have used and adapted the language of moral injury to describe the recognition of this anti-life logic of war in the world and how this recognition brings about despair in individuals. I began this book, however, attempting to say something about goodness and justice—they are somehow "revealed" through their absence in the war. That is to say, this work has been an effort to describe an awareness of and a desire for goodness and justice even in the midst of war, an effort to advocate for goodness and justice in the world and for people—not an argument for despair. The previous pages have included much despair; however, one must despair of the logic of death to encounter the mystery of life. Underneath the logic of war and death there remains life, that which was always there. As Emmanuel Lévinas puts it: "War can be produced [. . .] only where discourse was possible. [. . .] Violence can aim only at a face."[2]

In this chapter, I bring together several themes I have been developing throughout the book. Chapters 3 and 4 dealt with moral injury as a despair of the world and of one's self, leaving one in a place of turning. In affirming the logic of war and one's place in that logic as meaningless, one's sense of world and self has crumbled. This disintegration of meaning is driven by a desire for life—life that has been obscured and covered over by the framework of meaning that is already falling away as one despairs of it. One longs for something new as the old passes away. The site of disintegration and longing comprises the negative revelation at the heart of this book. This chapter serves as an analysis of negative revelation.

MAJOR CONCEPTS

As I flesh out the concept of negative revelation, I must first make explicit and distinguish major concepts to which I have been alluding.

The first major concept, which has been given the most attention in the previous pages, is *anti-life*. Anti-life is a false reality, a totalizing claim or vision of what is real and what is good. In chapter 1, I defined anti-life as *a static, parasitic, explanatory assault on the inexhaustible mystery of life that masquerades as life itself*. In chapter 2, I showed how the global war on terror is a form of anti-life through its totalizing lenses of full spectrum dominance, American sovereignty, and a pretense of moral superiority. Chapters 3 and 4 described the recognition of anti-life as an individual's despair of world and self, reworking the concept of moral injury.

The second major concept is *revelation* itself, and here I mean revelation in the sense of receiving some new and surprising positive content. This kind of revelation is like "seeing the light"; the good is disclosed. Such a revelation is often accompanied by some type of *metanoia*, a conversion, repentance, transformation, change of heart, or turning toward the good that has been revealed. This sort of revelation is *positive revelation*. Positive revelation is a vision of the good; it is a "mountaintop" experience. A famous twentieth-century example of positive revelation is that which drove Martin Luther King Jr. to speak with courage at the Bishop Charles Mason Temple the night before he was murdered, closing his address by responding to the fear of threats in Memphis, Tennessee:

> Well, I don't know what will happen now. We've got some difficult days ahead. But it doesn't matter with me now. Because I've been to the mountaintop. And I don't mind. Like anybody, I would like to live a long life. Longevity has its place. But I'm not concerned about that now. I just want to do God's will. And He's allowed me to go up to the mountain. And I've looked over. And I've seen the promised land. I may not get there with you. But I want you to know tonight, that we, as a people will get to the promised land. And I'm happy, tonight. I'm not worried about anything. I'm not fearing any man. Mine eyes have seen the glory of the coming of the Lord.[3]

I quote Martin Luther King Jr. at length because his writings are replete with positive revelation. James Washington's introduction to King's collected writings names King the "martyred prophet for a global beloved community of justice, faith, and hope."[4] King spoke against anti-life constructs of racism, classism, and militarism through his vision of a beloved community, the promised land, the "glory of the coming of the Lord." King and the Civil Rights movement encountered and confronted the forces of anti-life with a positive content, a vision of the good and the just, a way the world should be. They knew what the promised land looked like, even if they were not yet there.

The third concept is *negative revelation*. Negative revelation, quite simply, is the recognition that anti-life does not equal positive revelation. Anti-life masquerades as life, claiming the position of positive revelation for itself. Anti-life claims to be the good, claims truth. Recalling Origen: "For they think that justice is to do evil to the evil and good to the good; that is, according to their meaning, that one who is just will not show himself well disposed to the evil, but will behave towards them with a kind of hatred."[5] Recognizing that what has been described as goodness is in reality a kind of hatred is *not* to receive a positive revelation. The good is not disclosed through hatred. Anti-life is not life. Anti-life's claim on what is good is not the good. Anti-life's truth is a lie. Negative revelation is the disintegration of the meaning of anti-life for one's world and self, *without yet any new positive content in its place*. Negative revelation is beginning to wake from an anti-life nightmare, with no clear vision or dream of the beloved community to which one can yet cling. As with positive revelation, there is something attendant with negative revelation that is like a conversion, a transformation, a change of heart—but this conversion is incomplete. The space of negative revelation represents a turning point where one has rejected anti-life and longs for life—longs for some positive revelation of the good. There is a turning from, and a turning toward, but the turn toward is a turn toward *that which is not known*. This turning point is a relinquishing of knowing and claims to certainty, representing an openness to life and learning. With no vision from the mountaintop, one hopes to learn of that which could be seen from its height.

THE EXAMPLE OF SAUL/PAUL

I turn briefly to the story of Paul (known also as Saul) in the New Testament, as his transformation or change of heart involves both kinds of revelation, positive and negative—and his story helps me distinguish the two. In his letter to the churches of Galatia, Paul describes his own experience as a kind of positive revelation; he receives a vision and a teaching from God to take to the world: "For I want you to know, brothers and sisters, that the gospel that was proclaimed by me is not of human origin; for I did not receive it from a human source, nor was I taught it, but I received it through a revelation of Jesus Christ" (Galatians 1:11–12, NRSV). Paul's turning from persecuting followers of the Way involves a disclosure of the good to Paul—something for him to turn toward

> when God, who had set me apart before I was born and called me through his grace, was pleased to reveal his Son to me, so that I might proclaim him among the Gentiles, I did not confer with any human being, nor did I go up to Jerusalem to those who were already apostles before me, but I went away at once into Arabia, and afterwards I returned to Damascus. (Galatians 1:15–17)

As Paul turns toward his new life of teaching and proclaiming to the Gentiles, he writes of that turning as a moment when he was given clarity of purpose, a confidence in the content he had been given and his own role in proclaiming that content.

The story of Paul's turning is told somewhat differently by the author of Acts. Elements of positive revelation remain: a "light from heaven flashed around him" and the voice of Jesus addresses Saul directly (Acts 9:3–6). However, in this version of the story, Saul loses his sight: "Saul got up from the ground, and though his eyes were open, he could see nothing; so they led him by the hand and brought him into Damascus. For three days he was without sight, and neither ate nor drank" (Acts 9:8–10). Saul's sight is restored when Ananias (instructed in a vision to do so) lays hands on him: "'Brother Saul, the Lord Jesus, who appeared to you on your way here, has sent me so that you may regain your sight and be filled with the Holy Spirit.' And immediately something like scales fell from his eyes, and his sight was restored" (Acts 9:17–18). Saul/Paul's loss and restoration of sight is the element in the story of his turning that resembles negative revelation. He is incapable of doing anything after his encounter with a light and a voice; others must lead him. Another must restore him. When he is restored, he lives in the world differently. The book of Acts goes on to recount his journeys and proclamations, but before his journey and his proclamations he had to be "led by the hand." "Something like scales" fell from his eyes, and this is akin to the disintegration of anti-life's claim on the good. The old system of meaning crumbles and falls away.

In Paul's version of the story to the Galatians, he gets straight to work spreading the gospel after his turning, because some positive content has been revealed or disclosed to him. That is not the story I am telling with negative revelation. Negative revelation is not "seeing the light," or seeing

Jesus, or hearing the voice of God directly. The version in Acts is closer to negative revelation. Though he sees a light, Paul cannot understand it at first. He is helpless and lost; Paul's story *does* contain elements of negative revelation, in that the disintegration of meaning leaves him incapacitated for a time.

One of the most important elements of Paul's story as it is told in Acts (and most germane to this work) is that the restoration of his sight requires Ananias to lay hands on him. Ananias is a follower of the Way, a member of the group persecuted by Saul. Paul had not set out on the road to Damascus to receive a revelation of any sort, but rather: "still breathing threats and murder against the disciples of the Lord, went to the high priest and asked him for letters to the synagogues at Damascus, so that if he found any who belonged to the Way, men or women, he might bring them bound to Jerusalem" (Acts 9:1–2). It is important to note that this story has often been read as Paul's "conversion" from Judaism to Christianity. I am convinced by Pamela Eisenbaum's study of Paul that he "lived and died a Jew."[6] It is evident that Paul had a life changing experience; it is *not* evident that this change was about Paul renouncing Judaism. Paul is not ashamed of Judaism; it is his persecution of the church that "appears to be the only behavior of which Paul feels shame."[7] The point for me is that Paul receives his restoration at the hands of a person against whom he was "breathing threats and murder." I read Acts and Paul's own words in Galatians as a revelatory turning, not from one religion to another, but a turning from persecution to receiving and teaching. Saul/Paul was struck down, struck blind, and found himself at a turning point where he was open to receive something from the hands of another. It is precisely the openness in this encounter and the falling away of "something like scales" that comprises negative revelation.

THE REVELATION OF THE OTHER

Goodness and justice are concrete relational realities, not abstract concepts. Goodness and justice involve other beings. Morality happens, is founded, when I encounter another being who resists and exceeds my ideas that seek to comprehend her. In Lévinas's words:

> The idea of the perfect is not an idea but desire; it is the welcoming of the Other, the commencement of moral consciousness, which calls in question my freedom. [. . .] Conscience welcomes the Other. It is the revelation of a resistance to my powers that does not counter them as a greater force, but calls in question the naïve right of my powers. [. . .] Morality begins when freedom, instead of being justified by itself, feels itself to be arbitrary or violent.[8]

The problem with the global war on terror is that it put an idea of "morality" in the place of ethical encounter with Other(s). I brought this "morality" (anti-life) with me when I went to war. Anti-life comprised the context of war in which I encountered others. I did not know that it was anti-life. To borrow Bonhoeffer's language, this morality of war was an evil appearing "in the form of light, of beneficence, of faithfulness, of renewal . . . in the form of historical necessity."[9] War fixes scales over one's eyes, obscuring ethical relationships where genuine morality is founded.

A death-dealing component of the logic of war, the scales fixed over one's eyes, is the way people are replaced with ideas and concepts. I examined this conceptual determination of human beings in chapter 2. One striking example of this death-dealing logic is the application of the term "unlawful enemy combatant," in which detainees suspected of terrorism were denied any rights under the Geneva Conventions.[10] The term "unlawful enemy combatant" makes an ontological claim that short-circuits and renders moot questions of goodness and justice that arise in the encounter with other beings. The question "How shall an unlawful enemy combatant be treated?" is already answered by the term itself. "Unlawful enemy combatant" equals a person without rights, and that person can be treated however is most expedient for national security and the continued demonstration of U.S. power. In an unconventional war like the global war on terror, those who fight against the United States and its allies are by virtue of their resistance deemed terrorists, non-state actors, insurgents, unlawful. The Iraqi government and military were laid to waste as part of its "liberation." Thus, no one who could be construed as fighting the U.S. presence in Iraq could be acting on behalf of the state of Iraq; they were "unlawful"—counted as non-persons.

"Unlawful enemy combatant" is just one example of the way *ideas* began to take the place of *people* in the U.S. response to the destruction of the World Trade Center. An extensive vocabulary of ideas came to describe a new world after 9/11/2001: patriotism, terrorism, homeland defense, threat levels, national security, global war, terrorist cells, preemptive strikes, and so on; such new or redefined ideas became commonplace in everyday conversation in the United States. The global war on terror was itself a war against an idea rather than a nation or people. I am not claiming that the World Trade Center was not violently destroyed in an act of aggression—terrorism, even. I am saying that in response to the attack, the United States redefined the world to go to war with it. It is horrifyingly simple to summarize the foreign policy of the United States in the twenty-first century: we will kill, by any means necessary, every terrorist we can—but never people. We will do so with "boots on the ground" if necessary—boots that become heroes and martyrs in death, boots that are trotted out for celebrations and political rallies—but never by putting actual people at risk.

This is an upside-down world of anti-life. It is a world in which people are hidden and obscured by ideas of people. It is a world riddled with death, but where death becomes a number and a matter of debate. One can barely draw breath from the sea of ideas to speak honestly about what has occurred in this world under the guise of freedom and security. One cannot escape the apparatus of the war to talk about it. One finds oneself contained in a category—"veteran," "refugee," "activist," "suspect," "wounded warrior," "traitor." The machinery of war in our age, this evil in the form of light and historical necessity, keeps churning death and manufacturing new ideas to contain any who try to resist it. Whatever one's position, the anti-life logic of war has a name and idea ready at hand to render a person into a category. The anti-life logic of war levels the world into a static plane, a comprehensive ontology melting people down to a smooth, glass frame displaying the image of war: everything and everyone within the image (the world) can be defined by the terminology of war. In this way, war functions as a "totality" as Emmanuel Lévinas describes: "a casting into movement of beings hitherto anchored in their identity, a mobilization of absolutes, by an objective order from which there is no escape. [. . .] The meaning of individuals (invisible outside of this totality) is derived from the totality."[11]

I am arguing, in the spirit of Lévinas, that the global demonstration of military power by the United States in the twenty-first century is a kind of totalizing gaze; allies and enemies are comprehended and grasped, unified into a system that makes its own sense of the world through war. With the global war on terror, the United States mobilized an objective order, a totalizing ontology, that attempted to make sense of everything.

According to Lévinas, "ontology as first philosophy is a philosophy of power. It issues in the State and in the non-violence of the totality, without securing itself against the violence from which this non-violence lives, and which appears in the tyranny of the State."[12] War is obviously violent. I understand the "non-violence of the totality" here to refer to the ways ontology reconciles tension, in a philosophical sense, by making sense of all that exists under the rubric of "being" in general. Lévinas is taking up a nuanced argument with Heidegger, the intricacies of which distracts from my project. However, I read Lévinas saying that much of Western philosophy and the apparatus of the State are both threatened by alterity/otherness. Lévinas uses the phrase "primacy of the same" to show how ontology (in philosophy and in the State) "comprehends" and "neutralizes" otherness: "The neutralization of the other who becomes a theme or an object [. . .] is precisely his reduction to the same. [. . .] To know [ontologically] amounts to grasping being out of nothing or reducing it to nothing, removing from it its alterity."[13] Ontological knowing is relation with nothing other than "I," the same, myself: "The relation with Being that is enacted as ontology consists in neutralizing the existent in order to comprehend or grasp it. It is hence not a relation with the other as such but the reduction of the other to the same."[14] Lévinas continues: "*Being* before the *existent*, ontology before metaphysics, is freedom (be it the freedom of theory) before justice. It is a movement within the same before obligation to the other."[15] For example, "unlawful enemy combatant" describes *what kind of being* a person is, on terms decided from a perspective removed from any encounter between beings. "Soldier" and "insurgent," "combatant" and "noncombatant"—these are ways of integrating actual existents (people, in this case) into a system that comprehends them—what Lévinas calls a totality.

I remember the destruction of the World Trade Center, and I remember the way it did not seem to make any sense at all. With ontological tools ready at hand, the United States quickly "made sense" of it. Good and evil, freedom and security, war and terror, shock and awe, peace through strength, and so on are terms expressing tensions and conflicts that are "resolved" in ontological totality. Recalling President Bush's remarks at the 2002 West Point commencement: "We are in a conflict between good and evil, and America will call evil by its name. By confronting evil and lawless regimes, we do not create a problem, we reveal a problem. And we will lead the world in opposing it."[16] Again, I am not equating Bush with totalitarian dictators. However, the quote demonstrates clearly what I am taking pains to distill from Lévinas. America here has the power to name and to disclose: to comprehend the world by dividing it into good and evil. The philosophical conflict is resolved in the simplest of forms in that "evil" is in strict dialectic tension with "good." "Evil" here does not mean something radically other, it is a term that makes the other into the same. That is, "good and evil" grasps/comprehends the world as a system resolved in the totality of war. "Good" goes to war with "evil" to maintain "freedom." Real lives in their concrete multiplicity can be reduced and plugged into this system ad infinitum. This is the "freedom of theory" preceding questions of justice. The ontological designation of "evil" silences the question of justice before it can be asked.

Recalling Donald Rumsfeld once again, when Errol Morris asked, "How do you know when you're going too far?" Rumsfeld replied:

> You can't know with certainty. All the easy decisions are made down below. When you say, "How can you know?" the answer is you can't. Wouldn't it be wonderful if we could see around corners? [. . .to] have our imaginations anticipate every conceivable thing that could happen and then from that full array and spectrum, pick out the ones that will happen[17]

Donald Rumsfeld is not a straw person for my argument. In his wish for a kind of omniscience, he is echoing the aim of much of Western philosophy.

His answer reflects the "primacy of the same" in ontological knowing. In his wish, the world is pulled into his imagination, illuminated and comprehended. Rumsfeld's thinking here parallels Lévinas's description of Socrates: "primacy of the same was Socrates's teaching; to receive nothing of the Other but what is in me, as though from all eternity I was in possession of what comes to me from the outside—to receive nothing, or to be free."[18] To be fair to Rumsfeld, what secretary of defense welcomes surprise from the outside, especially the surprise of an attack on civilians? However, the apparatus of the global war on terror is put into place to neutralize the threat of surprise with the machinery of domination (described as full spectrum dominance, American sovereignty, and a pretense of moral superiority in chapter 2); "justice" becomes something like ontological knowing. The world and beings are reduced to an objectified grid. The effort robs the world of alterity. Borrowing Rumsfeld's terminology, the global war on terror strives to place everything and everyone into the category of "known knowns"—or to render all intelligible.

We must be able to name. Lévinas does not throw out ontology; however, he argues that "preexisting the plane of ontology is the ethical plane."[19] Countering totality and a comprehensive objectivity, Lévinas writes of transcendence and inexhaustible infinity. Preceding all totalizing efforts of comprehension is a situation of immediacy: "the immediate is the face to face."[20] Ideas can never catch up to this immediacy: "The way in which the other presents himself, exceeding *the idea of the other in me*, we here name face. [. . .] The face of the Other at each moment destroys and overflows the plastic image it leaves me, the idea existing to my own measure."[21]

The face of the Other in Lévinas's work is a revelation unto itself, and revelation is distinguished from disclosure: "*The absolute experience is not disclosure but revelation*: a coinciding of the expressed with him who expresses, which is the privileged manifestation of the Other, the manifestation of a face over and beyond form" (italics in original).[22] The face of the Other disrupts the category of "known knowns" and the vocabulary of war. The face expresses itself and is thus always a step ahead of ideas attempting to comprehend and neutralize the Other.

The ethical relation Lévinas describes in the face-to-face encounter between "I" and "Other" comprises language, discourse, and teaching; these concepts are summarized in "conversation": "*The other qua other is the Other*. To 'let him be' the relationship of discourse is required; pure 'disclosure,' where he is proposed as a theme, does not respect him enough for that. *We call justice this face to face approach, in conversation*."[23] In welcoming the face of the Other, I am taught; however, this teaching is revelation, not disclosure. The Other teaches from a "dimension of height," "beyond the system," "not on the same plane as myself."[24]

Two passages from Lévinas succinctly point toward goodness and justice, in a way that is germane to my development of negative revelation:

> [The] Other forever escapes knowing, but that there is no meaning in speaking here of knowledge or ignorance, for justice, the preeminent transcendence and the condition for knowing, is nowise [. . .] a noesis correlative of a noema.[25]
>
> [. . .]
>
> In contradistinction to plastic manifestation or disclosure, which manifests something *as* something, and in which the disclosed renounces its originality. [. . . The] presentation of the exterior being nowise referred to in our world is what we have called the face. And we have described the relation with the face that presents itself in speech as desire—goodness and justice.[26]

I read these passages alongside my three major concepts outlined in the beginning of this chapter. Goodness and justice are relational concepts, involving an Other(s). Morality happens, is founded, when I encounter the Other. What does the Other demand of me in ethical relation? What does the face of the Other teach me? The problem: I brought a "morality" (anti-life) with me to this encounter. Anti-life is the context of war in which I encounter. I did not know that it was anti-life. This morality appeared in the form of light. I thought I had a grasp of the good (positive revelation), but the grasp is the grasp of anti-life. The "morality" of anti-life and war situates the Other as an object that can be known, utterly comprehended, a "noesis correlative of a noema." This is not the language of justice.

The encounter with the Other *as Other being*, not as an idea of being—that is, an encounter with Other that opens a *dimension of height*, open to *teaching*, disrupts and destroys the morality (anti-life) I brought with me putting me and the arbitrariness of my freedom to question. This calling into question of my freedom is the very foundation of morality. The false morality must fall like "scales" from one's eyes to found morality. Like Saul/Paul, one must be "led by the hand."

This encounter with the Other sparks the event I am calling "negative revelation." The face of the Other teaches me, it reveals that anti-life is not life, is not light (positive revelation). This encounter does not give me "positive revelation," the good disclosed. It will never give me this so long as goodness means for me something like comprehension and disclosure. The Other is not graspable in this way. The Other cannot be spoken of in the language of "known knowns." In conversation, discourse, teaching, and expression, the Other always exceeds what I know about the Other, cannot be contained by my idea of Other. The Other breaks open, from a dimension of height, the category of "insurgent." In so doing, the Other breaks me out of the category of "soldier."

Something about this changes the way I think of the good. It is not given, grasped, or comprehended. Negative revelation strips anti-life away, like "scales" from the eyes. What I see is not the 'truth,' as in a truth comprehended. The good is not disclosed. Goodness and justice are situated in the ethical relation, in conversation, in the expression of the Other whose expression is always new. Every idea and claim on the good I have is exceeded in each moment of expression, each moment of discourse. As Lévinas states: "War can be produced [. . .] only where discourse was possible. [. . .] Violence can aim only at a face."[27] War is an attempt to silence the expression of the Other, whereas "justice is a right to speak."[28]

Consider this description of a typical U.S. convoy in Iraq, taken from David Finkel's narrative non-fiction work, *The Good Soldiers*:

> They moved past some children herding goats. They moved past a man pushing a block of concrete. They moved past a man smoking a cigarette and looking under the raised hood of a stalled car, and maybe the car really was stalled or maybe it was a car bomb that was about to explode. The soldiers slowed to a near stop. The man didn't acknowledge them. No one did. No one smiled at them. No one threw flowers. No one waved.
>
> Now someone did: a young boy dragging a piece of wire. He paused to wave at Kauzlarich, and Kauzlarich saw him and waved back, and what Kauzlarich saw was a waving boy who for all he knew was wired to explode, and what the boy saw was a thick window and a soldier behind it in body armor waving a hand that was encased in a glove.

Suspicion in 360 degrees—this is what four years of war had led to.[29]

Throughout this book, I have claimed that in war goodness and justice are somehow revealed in their absence. By "absence," I mean to say that the face of the Other is obscured by the "suspicion in 360 degrees" that years of war put in place. What we see through the grid of war is not goodness, nor justice. We see objects of suspicion, weighing them, attempting to comprehend them. We see gloves, body armor, thick windows, exploding boys; and, we are seen as such. This is the anti-life context in which we are supposed to do "good" for the world.

What I am trying to say with the language of negative revelation: *I do not know the good; I long for it.* And *longing for the good* is as far as I can go—I am weary of claims of *knowing*. The point I am trying to make here is simple: the real lives of real people exist, and they matter. There is an ethical relationship between living beings that precedes anti-life constructs, an encounter with others that does not construe them as objects of knowledge to be entered into the calculations of war's logic. The ethical relation between human beings precedes the ontological terms of war. While this is perhaps a simple observation, the negative revelation—the life of another breaking through anti-life constructs in the expression of the face—is the catalyst for a profound shift in thinking and being, venturing out from a self and world defined by war (of which one despairs) toward something new.

In the sections that follow, I will be turning to two Christian theologians: Friedrich Schleiermacher and Dietrich Bonhoeffer. Before doing so, I want to explicitly acknowledge, in order to respect, the Jewishness of Emmanuel Lévinas. Lévinas distinguished his religious and philosophical writings, but he was not allergic to writing about the divine philosophically.[30] Moreover, throughout *Totality and Infinity*, which is the primary work I have been citing, Lévinas alludes to the Other as "the stranger, the widow, and the orphan"— the language of the Hebrew Bible. At his prime, Lévinas was delivering commentaries on the Talmud as well as philosophical lectures.[31] Jonathan Burroughs notes that Lévinas used separate publishers to keep separate his "general philosophy" from his "more confessional writings" (Lévinas's own description of his work), but Burroughs convincingly argues that Lévinas's writings "exhibit a continuity and interrelatedness that limit the possibility of a strict distinction between the two."[32] As I put Lévinas in dialogue with Schleiermacher and Bonhoeffer, I am not claiming that he is a Christian theologian in disguise as a Jewish philosopher, or that Schleiermacher and Bonhoeffer are Jewish philosophers in disguise as Christian theologians. I want to acknowledge the alterity of these thinkers, that they were formed in distinct contexts and circumstances that are present in their work. I draw on them because they help me describe negative revelation and an encounter with the Other, and I do see points of resonance in their thinking, to which I now turn.

TURNING POINT

In this section, I turn briefly to the sections of Friedrich Schleiermacher's *The Christian Faith* that deal with the doctrine of regeneration. My motivation is to provide a thick description of a turning point, out of concern for persons despairing of self and world. I suggest that this turning point offers an account of living into the future with hope, without denying the past.

There is a point of connection between Lévinas and Schleiermacher: the language of *immediacy*. For Lévinas: "The immediate is the face to face."[33] For Schleiermacher, there is "immediate self-consciousness," the pious expression of which is the cornerstone of all religious affect, a feeling of "absolute dependence."[34] Both thinkers are writing, from different vantage points, of something *primordial*, something that precedes the realm of cognition or "known knowns," though not absent from cognition. Before turning more deeply into Schleiermacher, I wish to point out this resonance with Lévinas. Schleiermacher is explicitly using language of God and Christ, as one would expect in reading *The Christian Faith*. Lévinas on the Other should not be misconstrued to mean Lévinas on "God," but Lévinas does open the realm of religion, philosophically, in a way that is not incompatible with Schleiermacher's "feeling of absolute dependence." Transcendence, according to Lévinas, "designates a relation with a reality infinitely distant from my own reality, yet without this distance destroying this relation and without this relation destroying this distance, as would happen with relations within the same."[35] Furthermore, to be "I" for Lévinas presupposes a primordial relationship with Other: "to produce oneself as I—is to apprehend oneself with the same gesture that already turns toward the exterior to extra-vert and to manifest—to respond for what it apprehends—to express; it is to affirm that the becoming-conscious is already language."[36] Lastly, in a rare instance of explicit "God" language in *Totality and Infinity*: "Society with God is not an addition to God nor a disappearance of the interval that separates God from the creature. By contrast with totalization we have called it religion."[37] All I wish to say here is that Schleiermacher's religion in general terms, "a sense and taste for the Infinite in the finite"[38] and becoming conscious of ourselves as "absolutely dependent," resonates with Lévinas's idea of infinity and relation with an Other who is infinitely distant—where *relation* and *distance* do not negate one another. This primordial feeling, this ethical relation, precedes the cognitive logic of war that attempts to reduce, comprehend, and grasp other beings.

How is this primordial feeling relevant for the conversation about moral injury, a despair of the world and oneself? I return briefly to the medical model to illustrate what Schleiermacher has to contribute to the way I have been developing negative revelation and moral injury. Brett Litz and a team of scholars and clinicians, in their recently developed "adaptive disclosure" therapy, open a space for theology. In specific regard to the treatment of moral injury, "adaptive disclosure" utilizes novel "breakout sessions" in which a veteran or service member engages in an "evocative imaginal 'confession' and dialogue with a compassionate and forgiving moral authority in order to begin to challenge and address the shame and self-handicapping that accompany [morally injurious experiences]."[39] To be clear, in this therapeutic technique it is the compassionate and forgiving moral authority that is imagined; the dialogue actually takes place in the session—with the patient and sometimes the therapist providing the voice of the moral authority. However, Litz et al. admit: "It may be that a discussion with *an actual moral authority figure* is warranted. [. . .] The hope is that faith, communion with, and empathy from others who share a faith, and messages based on 'good' theology—centered on love and forgiveness—will help heal injuries over time."[40]

I am an advocate for love and forgiveness. However, there is a turn taken toward the past by the authors of *Adaptive Disclosure* that is representative, in my view, of much of the current discourse on moral injury. There is an attempt to *reclaim* the old. In the authors' words: "If we could, we would want service members and veterans harmed by war traumas to reclaim the person they were at the peak of their military service, as well as how potent, hopeful, and positive they may have been."[41] One example provided for how the therapist might sum up the dialogue at the end of a session is to encourage the patient to "reclaim some of who [she was] before, as well as keeping the best of what [she has] learned from being a service member and being in combat."[42] When the patient has overly defined herself by the morally injurious event, feeling "unforgiven and unforgiveable," the event needs to be separated from "the totality of self" and the patient needs to reengage with "premorbid values."[43] Chapter 3 of *Adaptive Disclosure* seeks to describe the "military culture and warrior ethos," including the military values instilled in service members (e.g., leadership, duty, honor, etc.), in a way that is approachable for civilians and clinicians.[44] As an Army veteran, I believe the authors execute this task quite well. However, there is a claim within that brings the difference of my view on moral injury into sharp contrast: "Fighters are what they are, so to try to become something else means a great loss."[45]

While seeking to reclaim/reconstruct the identity of a warrior/fighter may have something to offer those who still find some value in the military ethos, I suggest that there is another type of veteran who wishes to have nothing more to do with the values and culture instilled by the military—a veteran who sees becoming something other than a fighter not as a great loss but as a great *gain*. I do not feel obligated to argue at length that such a veteran exists; I am one. One aspect of moral injury, I contend, is seeing one's values in the military find their end or *telos* in an unjust war. There is a schism between goodness/justice and the warrior ethos one has taken on in the military. It is difficult, after having participated in war—the *telos* of a warrior ethos—to then wish to reach back into the past before the war and take on the very values that got one there in the first place. In my case, I wish to get as much distance as possible between life now and life in war, including the warrior values one takes on in training for war. This is, precisely, what Schleiermacher offers in the conversation—a description of the possibility of a *new* life and the cessation of the old.

With adaptive disclosure, the person with moral injury has entered a morbid state, perceiving herself as defined by a particular event and deserving of indefinite punishment. Part of what overcoming that perception includes, in therapies such as adaptive disclosure, is going *backward* from the event into the past and reclaiming herself at her "peak." I draw on the theology of Schleiermacher to put forward a different trajectory: the individual has come to a turning point in which the *past* is that which is morbid—a direction in which she no longer wishes to travel. She longs for a new direction—a new *life*, no less.

Schleiermacher provides a theological framework of the "primordial feeling" underneath/beyond the logic of war, of which one despairs, that serves as the catalyst for living into a future characterized by hope. In a section of his *Christian Faith* on "conversion," a concept falling under the larger umbrella of the doctrines of "regeneration" and "sanctification," Schleiermacher provides a brief, though rich, description of a "turning point." He defines every "turning point" as simultaneously "the end of one direction taken and the beginning of the direction taken over against it."[46] The turning point itself is not characterized by movement:

> The turning point between the two directions itself comprises a twofold lack of activity in the form of a no-more-being-active regarding the first direction taken and a not-yet-being active regarding the new direction taken. Hence, in lieu of the vanishing activity nothing remains to the subject for supplying one's spiritually animated being except a passive echo of that former activity which is now carried in feeling and which with respect to the activity not yet begun, is but a longing, viewed as a passive presentiment.[47]

This two-fold inactivity, a passive *echo* and a *longing*, is a creative space, orienting the individual toward what is becoming while the activity of the individual has ceased. Here, in the creative space of the turning point, the individual's self-consciousness is entirely receptive, not moving in any direction or acting on any external object. This is not to say nothing is going on in this space; receptivity is not stasis.

The *passive echo* of the former activity/direction is understood as contrition—"expressive of the collective life of sin," and "it exists as the firm retention in one's self-consciousness of what has passed."[48] The *longing* for the new direction at the turning point is understood as the "change of heart," which itself is also two-fold: "a continuous rejection of the community of sinful life" and "a desire to take up whatever impetus proceeds from Christ."[49]

In an older translation of Schleiermacher's work, echo and longing are rendered as "regret" and "desire."[50] The language of *regret* and *desire*, I think, connects well with Lévinas on the foundation of morality, in which one's arbitrary freedom is "called into question"; "the freedom that can be ashamed of itself founds truth."[51] Regret and desire—an echo and rejection of what has passed, coupled with a longing to take up new impetus—is a creative space in which one no longer acts on the world and others from one's own understanding of goodness and justice (here the warrior ethos), but receives. It is the interval like Saul/Paul's recounted in Acts, in which he could no longer see and had to be led by the hand. Paul was not in a period of stasis, but rather in a period of receiving from the Other. I note again that Paul was not turning away from Judaism to "Christianity," which was not yet named as such. "Other than the obvious transition from being hostile to Jesus to becoming a follower, the biggest difference between the earlier and later Paul is that he went from being a persecutor of the 'church of God' to being a victim of persecution."[52] The turning for Paul is not about Judaism; Paul remained a Jew his entire life—albeit one that had disagreements with other Jews. The shift was more about Paul's relationship to Roman authority. Eisenbaum speculates, based on recent scholarship on Paul, that "Paul turned from persecutor to persecuted because he turned from having a complacent attitude toward the Romans to preaching a message of defiance."[53] In my own view (which is not that of a biblical scholar), Paul receives through encounter with the Other a recognition that the Roman status quo did not equal goodness or justice.

The creative space of the turning point, felt as regret and desire, is a shift from "seeing" and "acting" on the world and others as they are defined by war's terms. One regrets acting on the world through one's own impetus, one's own isolated conception of the good, and desires to take up an impetus from the Other—becomes open to being taught and led by the hand. Through encounter with the Other—which for a Christian may be described as encountering Christ—one despairs of the anti-life grid that robs self and other of uniqueness and alterity. These scales of "knowing" the world fall from one's eyes, and one enters a space where one's activity becomes receptivity—a desire for the Other which is the foundation of goodness and justice.

CONCLUSION: OPEN TO LIFE

In her recent work on life after trauma, Shelly Rambo states, "While there has been significant scholarship exposing the problem of the alliance between the Christian story and the American war story, there have been few attempts to reclaim the Christian story from the perspective of those who have been touched by war most closely."[54]

As a Christian theologian and a combat veteran, I want to conclude this work by making some attempt to reclaim the Christian story from war. I feel, at this point, that I have given enough space and words to anti-life and the American war story. The negative revelation I have been describing is not merely the recognition of anti-life, but a turn toward life. I wish to say something about life now.

During my years as a graduate student, I found a beloved theological conversation partner in Dietrich Bonhoeffer. In an outline for a book on which he was working in the last year of his life, in prison, Bonhoeffer wrote: "In the end it all comes down to the human being."[55]

Reclaiming the Christian story from the American war story is, in some ways, as simple as Bonhoeffer's statement: it really does come down to the human being. In the passage from which the quote is taken, Bonhoeffer was talking about the threat of totality, using the word "organization."[56] In the work of Lévinas, totality is breached in face-to-face conversation between "I" and "Other." Lévinas, a Jewish philosopher whose Lithuanian family was murdered by the Nazis, was not interested in the Christian story. Bonhoeffer was very much interested in the Christian story, and these last pages are my effort to show, using his work, how a Christian might arrive at some of the same conclusions as Lévinas—albeit with very different language.

I have referred often to the passage in Bonhoeffer's *Ethics* in which he discusses "evil in the form of light"—and how this renders the ethical "weapons" of our ancestors "insufficient for the present struggle." Bonhoeffer does not deride those old weapons, calling them "goods and convictions of a noble humanity." However, "it is the best, with all they are and can do, who thus go under."[57] This passage shook me when I first encountered it. I felt that it clearly captured everything wrong with the war—how we could be so "duped" by morality. Bonhoeffer argues that we must "replace rusty weapons with bright steel," and bright steel is "simplicity" and "wisdom":

> Only the person who combines simplicity with wisdom can endure. But what is simplicity? What is wisdom? How do the two become one? A person is simple who in the confusion, the distortion, and the inversion of all concepts keeps in sight only the single truth of God.
>
> [. . .] Not fettered by principles but bound by love for God, this person is liberated from the problems and conflicts of ethical decision, and is no longer beset by them. This person belongs to God and to God's will alone. The single-minded person does not also cast glances at the world while standing next to God and therefore is able, free and unconstrained, to see the reality of the world. Thus simplicity becomes wisdom. The person is wise who sees reality as it is, who sees into the depth of things. Only that person is wise who sees reality in God.[58]

The first time I read *this* passage, I was disappointed. Where Bonhoeffer had so precisely named the problems, the way the world was turned upside down, I felt he had prescribed only some vague, cryptic words about God as a solution. I do not know how to be simple and wise. I do not know how to keep only "the single truth of God in sight." People have told me my whole life to look to God; I ended up in Iraq fighting an anti-life war. For some time, Bonhoeffer became for me a conversation partner who could clearly articulate problems, but I felt that I would need to go elsewhere to reclaim the Christian story from war.

I have revisited my friend Bonhoeffer many times over the course of my education. He fascinates me. I fear, at times, that I have a kind of hero-worship going on. I believe my initial dissatisfaction with him was my own inward insistence on wanting to learn *how to be good*. According to Bonhoeffer, the good is not a question of "how," but of "who," and the answer to "who" is always Jesus Christ.[59] Because God became human in Jesus Christ, Jesus Christ is the "who" one can look toward to "fix one's eyes on God and the world together at the same time" (simplicity and wisdom): "Whoever looks at Jesus Christ sees in fact God and the world in one. From then on they can no longer see God without the world, or the world without God."[60] It is important to note that looking to Christ is *not* about principles and doctrines for Bonhoeffer—looking to Christ is about looking to the Other, a real and living human being:

> Christ is not a principle according to which the whole world must be formed. Christ does not proclaim a system of that which would be good today, here, and at all times. Christ does not teach an abstract ethic that must be carried out, cost what it may. Christ was not essentially a teacher, a lawgiver, but a human being, a real human being like us. [. . .] Christ did not, like an ethicist, love a theory about the good; he loved real people. Christ was not interested, like a philosopher, in what is "generally valid," but in that which serves real concrete human beings. [. . .] God did not become an idea, a principle, a program, a universally valid belief, or a law. God became human.[61]

In this passage, Bonhoeffer lays out quite plainly all the ways Christianity can fail as an anti-dote to anti-life. Principles, systems, abstractions, laws, universally valid beliefs—all may become fuel for the fodder. However, Bonhoeffer also gives us a Christianity that pierces anti-life: "he loved real people." Where Lévinas describes how the dimension of height is opened up in the face of the Other, Bonhoeffer describes the dimension of height taking on the face of the Other, loving the Other. Christ in this passage affirms human life by *living*—it is by the living Christ that anti-life is overturned. This life, this vitality, often obscured in Christianity as a system, is the only means by which the Christian story can be disentangled from the ancient lie now present as the American war story.

Christ, for Bonhoeffer, is the "humiliated and exalted One," much like Lévinas's Other: "The nakedness of the face is destituteness. To recognize the Other is to recognize a hunger. To recognize the Other is to give. But it is to give to the master, to the lord, to him whom one approaches as 'You' in a dimension of height."[62] Bonhoeffer also resonates with Lévinas on the topic of transcendence:

> Who is God? [. . .] Encounter with Jesus Christ. Experience that here there is a reversal of all human existence, in the very fact that Jesus only is there for others. Jesus's "being-for-others" is the experience of transcendence! [. . .] The transcendent is not the infinite, unattainable tasks, but the neighbor within reach in any given situation.[63]

According to Lévinas, to "enter into the straightforwardness of the face to face [. . .] places the center of gravitation of a being outside of that being."[64] Bonhoeffer wrote at length of Christ as the center of one's life, from his Christology lectures in Berlin in 1933 to the end of his life.[65] In his last year, in prison, Bonhoeffer wrote of faith as conversion in a way that, I believe, reclaims Christianity from any war story:

> I want to learn to have faith [. . .] one only learns to have faith by living in the full this-worldliness of life. If one has completely renounced making something of oneself—whether it be a saint or a converted sinner or a church leader (a so-called priestly figure!), a just or an unjust person, a sick or a healthy person—then one throws oneself completely into the arms of God, and this is what I call this-worldliness: living fully in the midst of life's tasks, questions, successes and failures, experiences, and perplexities—then one takes seriously no longer one's own sufferings but rather the suffering of God in the world. Then one stays awake with Christ in Gethsemane. And I think this is faith; this is metanoia. And this is how one becomes a human being, a Christian.[66]

Negative revelation is about trying so very hard to do what is good and just based on claims of goodness and justice that one believes to one's core, in which one is confident. Negative revelation is about learning that, as it turns out, what one thought one knew about goodness and justice was wrong. Goodness and justice are not ideas. The false claims on the good are disintegrated as one receives the expression of the face of the Other—the ethical relation in which goodness and justice reside, outside the realm of objective knowing and claims of certainty. In receiving from the expression of the Other, one desires to give—one wants to learn to have faith. To think of this in Christian terms is to stop thinking, in a sense. It is to let go of Christ as a principle and to meet Christ in this world, and in this life. Christianity is staying awake to the suffering of the other, being open to life. Openness to life does not renounce cognition, but renounces resting in cognition. Negative revelation is "knowing" that I do not know goodness and justice, and I cannot know. Negative revelation is turning from these disintegrated "known knowns" of anti-life, now an echoing of regret; turning in desire toward the face of the Other—of neighbor—of Christ—where goodness and justice are given and received as life.

NOTES

1. See Chapter 1. Whether we are "duped by morality" is the question with which Lévinas opens his *Totality and Infinity*, 21. The language of "contempt and idolization of human beings" comes from Dietrich Bonhoeffer, *Ethics*, ed. Clifford J. Green, trans. Reinhard Krauss, Charles C. West, and Douglas W. Stott, *Dietrich Bonhoeffer Works*, Vol. 6 (Minneapolis, MN: Fortress Press, 2005), 85.

2. Emmanuel Lévinas, *Totality and Infinity: An Essay on Exteriority* (Pittsburgh, PA: Duquesne University Press, 1969), 225.

3. Martin Luther King Jr., "I See the Promised Land," in *A Testament of Hope: The Essential Writings and Speeches of Martin Luther King, Jr.*, ed. James M. Washington (HarperOne, 1991), 286.

4. James M Washington, ed., *A Testament of Hope*, ix.

5. Origen, *On First Principles*, trans. G. W. Butterworth (Notre Dame, IN: Christian Classics, 2013), 125.

6. Pamela Michelle Eisenbaum, *Paul Was Not a Christian: The Original Message of a Misunderstood Apostle* (New York: HarperOne, 2009), 5.

7. Ibid., 42.

8. Lévinas, *Totality and Infinity*, 84.

9. Dietrich Bonhoeffer, *Ethics*, ed. Clifford J. Green, trans. Reinhard Krauss, Charles C. West, and Douglas W. Stott, *Dietrich Bonhoeffer Works*, Vol. 6 (Minneapolis, MN: Fortress Press, 2005), 77.

10. See *Military Commissions Act of 2006*, Public Law 109-366, *U.S. Statutes at Large* 120 (2006): 2600–37. See especially section 948b, "No alien unlawful enemy combatant subject to trial by military commission under this chapter may invoke the Geneva Conventions as a source of rights," accessed August 3, 2021, https://www.loc.gov/rr/frd/Military_Law/pdf/PL-109-366.pdf

11. Lévinas, *Totality and Infinity*, 21–22.

12. Ibid., 46.

13. Ibid., 43–44.

14. Ibid., 45–46.

15. Ibid., 47.

16. George W. Bush, "Commencement Address at the United States Military Academy in West Point, New York," *Weekly Compilation of Presidential Documents* 38, no. 2 (June 10, 2002): 944–48.

17. *The Unknown Known*, directed by Errol Morris (Anchor Bay Entertainment, 2014), accessed August 3, 2021, Amazon Prime Video, https://www.amazon.com/Known-Donald-Rumsfeld/dp/B00JGMJ914.

18. Lévinas, *Totality and Infinity*, 43.
19. Ibid., 201.
20. Ibid., 52.
21. Ibid., 50–51.
22. Ibid., 65–66.
23. Ibid., 71.
24. Ibid., 100, 171.
25. Ibid., 89–90.
26. Ibid., 296.
27. Ibid., 225.
28. Ibid., 298.
29. David Finkel, *The Good Soldiers* (New York: Picador, 2009), 40.
30. See, for example, Lévinas, *Totality and Infinity: An Essay on Exteriority*, 78–79. "The dimension of the divine opens forth from the human face. [. . .] The Other is the very locus of metaphysical truth, and is indispensable for my relation with God."
31. See Emmanuel Lévinas, *Nine Talmudic Readings*, translated by Annette Aronowicz (Bloomington, IN: Indiana University Press, 2019).
32. Jonathan Burroughs, "Emmanuel Lévinas' Methodological Approach to the Jewish Sacred Texts," *The Heythrop Journal* 53, no. 1 (January 2012): 124–36.
33. Lévinas, *Totality and Infinity*, 52.
34. A lengthy exposition of "immediate self-consciousness"—that "earlier moment [. . .] which you always experience yet never experience"—can be found in the second of Schleiermacher's speeches on religion: Friedrich Schleiermacher, *On Religion: Speeches to Its Cultured Despisers*, trans. John Oman, Westminster/John Knox Press (Louisville, KY: Westminster/John Knox Press, 1994), 26–118. Jack Forstman, in his Foreword to this edition of the *Speeches*, summarizes the second speech: "religion is neither a knowing nor a doing but something whose occasion or foundation touches a locus in the human being more fundamental than either knowing or doing. Schleiermacher describes this locus as 'feeling' and the occasion as 'a sense and taste for the Infinite in the finite'" (p. x, 39).

Schleiermacher further develops "immediate self-consciousness" in proposition (§) 3 of his *Glaubenslehre* (*Christian Faith*): "The piety that constitutes the basis of all ecclesial communities, regarded purely in and of itself, is neither a knowing nor a doing but a distinct formation of feeling, or of immediate self-consciousness." In §4, the expression of piety in general—before becoming concrete in particular religious communities—is the occasion in that locus of human being (immediate self-consciousness) in which "we are conscious of ourselves as absolutely dependent or, which intends the same meaning, as being in relation to God." Friedrich Schleiermacher, *Christian Faith : A New Translation and Critical Edition*, trans. Terrence N. Tice, Catherine L. Kelsey, and Edwina Lawler (Louisville, KY: Westminster John Knox Press, 2016), 8, 18.

35. Lévinas, *Totality and Infinity*, 41.
36. Ibid., 304.
37. Ibid., 104.

38. Schleiermacher, *On Religion*, 39.

39. Brett T. Litz, Leslie Lebowitz, Matt J. Gray, and William P. Nash, *Adaptive Disclosure : A New Treatment for Military Trauma, Loss, and Moral Injury* (New York: The Guilford Press, 2016), 5.

40. Ibid., 126.

41. Ibid., 93.

42. Ibid., 58–59.

43. Ibid., 87.

44. Ibid., 29–42.

45. Ibid., 41.

46. Friedrich Schleiermacher, *Christian Faith*, 694.

47. Ibid., 694.

48. Ibid., 695.

49. Friedrich Schleiermacher, *Christian Faith*, 696. The concept of contrition resonates with Reinhold Niebuhr's claim that an ironic situation "must dissolve, if men or nations are made aware of their complicity in it. Such awareness involves some realization of the hidden vanity or pretension by which comedy is turned into irony. This realization either must lead to an abatement of the pretension, which means contrition; or it leads to a desperate accentuation of the vanities to the point where irony turns into pure evil." Reinhold Niebuhr, *The Irony of American History* (Chicago: University of Chicago Press, 2008), xxiv. See also chapter 2.

50. Friedrich Schleiermacher, *The Christian Faith* (Philadelphia, PA: Fortress Press, 1976), 484.

51. Lévinas, *Totality and Infinity*, 83–84.

52. Eisenbaum, *Paul Was Not a Christian*, 143.

53. Ibid., 146.

54. Shelly Rambo, *Resurrecting Wounds: Living in the Afterlife of Trauma* (Waco, TX: Baylor University Press, 2017), 113.

55. Dietrich Bonhoeffer, *Letters and Papers from Prison*, ed. John W. de Gruchy, trans. Isabel Best et al., Dietrich Bonhoeffer Works, Vol. 8 (Minneapolis, MN: Fortress Press, 2010), 500.

> 56. "Nature used to be conquered by the soul; with us it is conquered through technological organization of all kinds. What is unmediated for us, what is given, is no longer nature but organization. But with this protection from the menace of nature, a new threat to life is created in turn, namely, through organization itself. Now the power of the What will protect us from the menace of organization? The human being is thrown back on his own resources. He has learned to cope with everything except himself. He can insure himself against everything but other human beings. In the end it all comes down to the human being."
>
> Bonhoeffer, *Letters and Papers from Prison*, 500.

57. Bonhoeffer, *Ethics*, 77–80.

58. Ibid., 81.

59. "The source of a Christian ethic is not the reality of one's own self, not the reality of the world, nor is it the reality of norms and values. It is the reality of God that is revealed in Jesus Christ." Bonhoeffer, *Ethics*, 81.

60. Bonhoeffer, *Ethics*, 81.

61. Ibid., 98–99. See also Dietrich Bonhoeffer, *Berlin: 1932–1933*, ed. Larry L. Rasmussen, trans. Isabel Best and David Higgins, Dietrich Bonhoeffer Works, Vol. 12 (Minneapolis, MN: Fortress Press, 2009), 303: "The 'who' question is the quintessential religious question. It is the question that asks about the other person, the other being, the other authority. It is the question of transcendence, of existence, is the question about the neighbor; it is the question about [being] a person."

62. Bonhoeffer, *Berlin: 1932–1933*, 310. Lévinas, *Totality and Infinity*, 75.

63. Bonhoeffer, *Letters and Papers from Prison*, 501.

64. Lévinas, *Totality and Infinity*, 183.

65. See Bonhoeffer, *Berlin: 1932–1933*, 324–5: "I am separated, by a boundary that I cannot cross, from the self that I ought to be. This boundary lies between my old self and my new self, that is, in the center between myself and me. As the limit, Christ is at the same time the center that I have regained." See Bonhoeffer, *Letters and Papers from Prison*, 366–67: "I'd like to speak of God not at the boundaries but in the center [. . .] God is the beyond in the midst of our lives."

66. Bonhoeffer, *Letters and Papers from Prison*, 486.

References

Allawi, Ali A. *The Occupation of Iraq: Winning the War, Losing the Peace*. New Haven, CT: Yale University Press, 2007.

Althaus-Reid, Marcella. *Indecent Theology: Theological Perversions in Sex, Gender, and Politics*. New York: Routledge, 2000.

Aquinas, Thomas. *The Summa Theologica of St. Thomas Aquinas: Complete English Edition in Five Volumes*. Translated by Fathers of the English Dominican Province. Vol. 2. Notre Dame, IN: Christian Classics, 1981.

Arendt, Hannah. *Eichmann in Jerusalem: A Report on the Banality of Evil*. New York: Penguin Books, 2006.

———. *The Origins of Totalitarianism*. New Edition with Added Prefaces. New York: Harcourt, Inc., 1994.

Barth, Karl. *Church Dogmatics III.3: The Doctrine of Creation*. Edited by G.W. Bromiley and T.F. Torrance. Translated by G.W. Bromiley and R.J. Ehrlich. New York: T&T Clark International, 2004.

Bonhoeffer, Dietrich. *Berlin: 1932–1933*. Edited by Larry L. Ramussen. Translated by Isabel Best and David Higgins. Dietrich Bonhoeffer Works, Vol. 12. Minneapolis, MN: Fortress Press, 2009.

———. *Creation and Fall : A Theological Exposition of Genesis 1–3*. Edited by John W. de Gruchy. Translated by Douglas Stephen Bax. Dietrich Bonhoeffer Works, Vol. 3. Minneapolis, MN: Fortress Press, 1997.

———. *Discipleship*. Edited by Geffrey B. Kelly and John D. Godsey. Translated by Barbara Green and Reinhard Krauss. Dietrich Bonhoeffer Works, Vol. 4. Minneapolis, MN: Fortress Press, 2001.

———. *Ethics*. Edited by Clifford J. Green. Translated by Reinhard Krauss, Charles C. West, and Douglas W. Stott. Dietrich Bonhoeffer Works, Vol. 6. Minneapolis, MN: Fortress Press, 2005.

———. *Letters and Papers from Prison*. Edited by John W. de Gruchy. Translated by Isabel Best, Lisa E. Dahill, Reinhard Krauss, and Nancy Lukens. Dietrich Bonhoeffer Works, Vol. 8. Minneapolis, MN: Fortress Press, 2010.

Boudreau, Tyler. "The Morally Injured." *Massachusetts Review* 52, no. 3/4 (2011): 746–54.
Brison, Susan J. *Aftermath: Violence and the Remaking of a Self.* Princeton, NJ: Princeton University Press, 2002.
Brock, Rita Nakashima, and Gabriella Lettini. *Soul Repair: Recovering from Moral Injury after War.* Boston, MA: Beacon Press, 2012.
Burroughs, Jonathan. "Emmanuel Levinas' Methodological Approach to the Jewish Sacred Texts." *The Heythrop Journal* 53, no. 1 (January 2012): 124–36.
Bush, George W. "A Period of Consequences." Speech at The Citadel, Charleston, South Carolina, September 23, 1999. http://www3.citadel.edu/pao/addresses/pres_bush.html.
———. "Address to the Nation on the Terrorist Attacks." *Weekly Compilation of Presidential Documents* 37, no. 37 (September 17, 2001): 1301–302.
———. "Commencement Address at the United States Military Academy in West Point, New York." *Weekly Compilation of Presidential Documents* 38, no. 2 (June 10, 2002): 944–48.
Chivers, C.J. *The Fighters: Americans in Combat in Afghanistan and Iraq.* New York: Simon and Schuster, 2018.
Cone, James. *A Black Theology of Liberation.* Fortieth Anniversary Edition. Maryknoll, NY: Orbis Books, 2016.
Cone, James H. *The Cross and the Lynching Tree.* Maryknoll, NY: Orbis Books, 2011.
Douglas, Kelly Brown. *Stand Your Ground: Black Bodies and the Justice of God.* Maryknoll, NY: Orbis Books, 2015.
Eisenbaum, Pamela Michelle. *Paul Was Not a Christian: The Original Message of a Misunderstood Apostle.* New York: HarperOne, 2009.
Farnsworth, Jacob K. "Is and Ought: Descriptive and Prescriptive Cognitions in Military-Related Moral Injury." *Journal of Traumatic Stress* 32, no. 3 (June 1, 2019): 373–81. doi: 10.1002/jts.22356.
Filkins, Dexter. *The Forever War.* New York: Vintage Books, 2009.
Finkel, David. *The Good Soldiers.* New York: Picador, 2009.
Graham, Bradley. *By His Own Rules: The Ambitions, Successes, and Ultimate Failures of Donald Rumsfeld.* New York: PublicAffairs, 2009.
Hedges, Chris. *War Is a Force That Gives Us Meaning.* New York: Anchor Books, 2003.
"Joint Vision 2020: America's Military—Preparing for Tomorrow." *Joint Force Quarterly*, no. 25 (Summer 2000): 57–76.
King Jr., Martin Luther. "I See the Promised Land." In *A Testament of Hope: The Essential Writings and Speeches of Martin Luther King, Jr.*, edited by James M. Washington. HarperOne, 1991.
Kinghorn, Warren. "Combat Trauma and Moral Fragmentation: A Theological Account of Moral Injury." *Journal of the Society of Christian Ethics* 32, no. 2 (2012): 57–74. http://dx.doi.org/10.1353/sce.2012.0041.
Lévinas, Emmanuel. *Totality and Infinity: An Essay on Exteriority.* Translated by Alphonso Lingis. Pittsburgh, PA: Duquesne University Press, 1969.

Litz, Brett T., Leslie Lebowitz, Matt J. Gray, and William P. Nash. *Adaptive Disclosure : A New Treatment for Military Trauma, Loss, and Moral Injury*. New York: The Guilford Press, 2016.

Litz, Brett T., Nathan Stein, Eileen Delaney, Leslie Lebowitz, William P. Nash, Caroline Silva, and Shira Maguen. "Moral Injury and Moral Repair in War Veterans: A Preliminary Model and Intervention Strategy." *Clinical Psychology Review* 29, no. 8 (December 2009): 695–706. doi: 10.1016/j.cpr.2009.07.003.

Logan, Drake, and Adele Carpenter. "Operation Recovery: Fort Hood Soldiers & Veterans Testify on the Right to Heal," 2014. https://www.ivaw.org/sites/default/files/documents/Ft%20Hood%20Report.pdf.

MacIntyre, Alasdair C. *After Virtue: A Study in Moral Theory*. Third edition. Notre Dame, IN: University of Notre Dame Press, 2007.

Meagher, Robert E. *Killing from the Inside Out : Moral Injury and Just War*. Eugene, OR: Cascade Books, 2014.

"Military Commissions Act of 2006." Public Law 109-366, U.S. Statutes at Large 120 Stat. 2600, 2006.

Moon, Zachary. *Warriors Between Worlds: Moral Injury and Identities in Crisis*. New York: Lexington Books, 2019.

Morris, Errol. *The Unknown Known*. Anchor Bay Entertainment, 2014. https://www.amazon.com/Known-Donald-Rumsfeld/dp/B00JGMJ9l4.

Niebuhr, H. Richard (Helmut Richard). *The Meaning of Revelation*. Louisville, KY: Westminster John Knox Press, 2006.

Niebuhr, Reinhold. *The Irony of American History*. Chicago: The University of Chicago Press, 2008.

Nussbaum, Martha C. "Finely Aware and Richly Responsible: Literature and the Moral Imagination." In *Love's Knowledge: Essays on Philosophy and Literature*, 148–67. New York: Oxford University Press, 1990.

———. *The Fragility of Goodness: Luck and Ethics in Greek Tragedy and Philosophy*. Revised edition. New York: Cambridge University Press, 2001.

O'Brien, Tim. *The Things They Carried*. Boston, MA: Mariner Books, 2009.

Origen. *On First Principles*. Translated by G. W. Butterworth. Notre Dame, IN: Christian Classics, 2013.

Powers, Brian S. *Full Darkness: Original Sin, Moral Injury, and Wartime Violence*. Grand Rapids, MI: William. B. Eerdmans Publishing Company, 2019.

Powers, Kevin. *The Yellow Birds: A Novel*. New York: Little, Brown and Company, 2012.

Rambo, Shelly. *Resurrecting Wounds : Living in the Afterlife of Trauma*. Waco, TX: Baylor University Press, 2017.

Ricks, Thomas E. *Fiasco: The American Military Adventure in Iraq*. New York: Penguin Books, 2006.

Rumsfeld, Donald. "Department of Defense News Briefing—Secretary Rumsfeld and General Myers." U.S. Department of Defense News Transcript, February 12, 2002. https://archive.defense.gov/Transcripts/Transcript.aspx?TranscriptID=2636.

———. *Known and Unknown: A Memoir*. New York: Sentinel, 2011.

———. *Rumsfeld's Rules: Leadership Lessons in Business, Politics, War, and Life.* New York: Broadside Books, 2013.

———. "Sovereignty and Anticipatory Self-Defense," August 24, 2002. https://www.rumsfeld.com/archives.

Rumsfeld, Donald H. Fox News Sunday, November 2, 2003. https://archive.defense.gov/Transcripts/Transcript.aspx?TranscriptID=2870.

Schleiermacher, Friedrich. *Christian Faith : A New Translation and Critical Edition.* Translated by Terrence N. Tice, Catherine L. Kelsey, and Edwina Lawler. Louisville, KY: Westminster John Knox Press, 2016.

———. *Christmas Eve Celebration: A Dialogue.* Edited and translated by Terrence N. Tice. Eugene, OR: Cascade Books, 2010.

———. *On Religion : Speeches to Its Cultured Despisers.* Translated by John Oman. Louisville, KY: Westminster/John Knox Press, 1994.

———. *The Christian Faith.* Edited by H.R. Mackintosh and J.S. Stewart. Philadelphia, PA: Fortress Press, 1976.

Shay, Jonathan. *Achilles in Vietnam : Combat Trauma and the Undoing of Character.* New York: Scribner, 1994.

———. "Moral Injury." *Psychoanalytic Psychology* 31, no. 2 (2014): 182–91. doi:10.1037/a0036090.

———. *Odysseus in America: Combat Trauma and the Trials of Homecoming.* New York: Scribner, 2002.

Stiltner, Brian. *Toward Thriving Communities: Virtue Ethics as Social Ethics.* Winona, MN: Anselm Academic, 2016.

Tillich, Paul. *Dynamics of Faith.* New York: Harper and Row, 1957.

———. *Systematic Theology: Volume One.* Chicago: University of Chicago Press, 1951.

———. *Systematic Theology: Volume Three.* Chicago: University of Chicago Press, 1963.

———. *The Courage to Be.* Third Edition. New Haven, CT: Yale University Press, 2014.

Tirman, John. *The Deaths of Others: The Fate of Civilians in America's Wars.* New York: Oxford University Press, 2011.

Tolkien, J. R. R. *The Lord of the Rings: 50th Anniversary, One Vol. Edition.* 50th Anniversary ed. edition. Boston, MA: Houghton Mifflin Harcourt, 2005.

———. *The Silmarillion.* Edited by Christopher Tolkien. Boston, MA: Houghton Mifflin Harcourt, 2001.

United States and White House Office. *The National Security Strategy of the United States of America.* Washington, DC: President of the U.S., 2002.

U.S. Department of Defense. "Casualty Status." Accessed April 17, 2020. https://www.defense.gov/casualty.pdf.

U.S. Supreme Court. "Hamdan vs. Rumsfeld, Syllabus, 548 U.S. 557," 2006.

Waggoner, Ed. *Religion in Uniform: A Critique of U.S. Military Chaplaincy.* New York: Lexington Books, 2019.

Walter, George. *The Penguin Book of First World War Poetry.* London: Penguin Classics, 2006.

Walzer, Michael. *Just and Unjust Wars: A Moral Argument with Historical Illustrations*. Fifth edition. New York: Basic Books, 2015.

Weil, Simone. "The Love of God and Affliction." In *Waiting for God*, 67–82. New York: Harper Perennial, 2001.

Wiinikka-Lydon, Joseph. "Moral Injury as Inherent Political Critique: The Prophetic Possibilities of a New Term." *Political Theology* 18, no. 3 (May 2017): 219–32. http://dx.doi.org/10.1080/1462317X.2015.1104205.

Yandell, Michael. "Do Not Torment Me: The Morally Injured Gerasene Demoniac." In *Moral Injury: A Guidebook for Understanding and Engagement*, edited by Brad Kelle. New York: Lexington Books, 2020.

Yeterian, Julie D., Danielle S. Berke, Jessica R. Carney, Alexandra McIntyre-Smith, Katherine St. Cyr, Lisa King, Nora K. Kline, Andrea Phelps, Brett T. Litz, and Members of the Moral Injury Outcomes Project Consortium. "Defining and Measuring Moral Injury: Rationale, Design, and Preliminary Findings from the Moral Injury Outcome Scale Consortium." *Journal of Traumatic Stress* 32, no. 3 (2019): 363–72. doi: 10.1002/jts.22380.

Index

9/11/2001, 1, 3–4, 77

adaptive disclosure, 109–10
Allawi, Ali A., 45
Althaus-Reid, Marcella, 4–8
American exceptionalism, 26, 31, 34
anti-life, 2, 6, 9, 11, 13–31, 35–42, 46–51, 53, 57, 59–62, 65–66, 69, 72, 77–78, 84, 91, 93, 97–103, 106–7, 112, 114; definition of, 18, 26, 31, 35, 98
Arendt, Hannah, 9, 17, 22–27, 30, 35–36, 50
Army Values, 81, 83–84, 90, 93, 110

Barth, Karl, 9, 17–22, 26
betrayal, 58–59, 61–71, 77–78, 92–93
Bonhoeffer, Dietrich, 2, 9, 11, 16, 26, 28–30, 33, 96n69, 108, 113–15, 118n55, 119n59, 65
Boudreau, Tyler, 65–66
Brison, Susan, 3, 11, 84–86, 92
Brock, Rita Nakashima, 3, 74n25
Burroughs, Jonathan, 108
Bush, George W., 1, 10–11, 35–36, 45–47, 49, 51, 62, 86–87, 104

Chivers, C.J., 1, 49, 89
Cone, James, 19–21, 23, 52
courage, 3, 15, 19, 21, 27, 80

deception, 5–6, 9, 26–28, 37, 53, 57, 59, 71, 97, 113, 116n1
despair, xi, 10–11, 17, 58–59, 61, 77–78, 90–91, 93, 97–98, 108–9, 111–12
dialectic, 18, 20–22, 104
disintegration, 2, 5, 11, 13, 84–85, 90, 97–101, 115–16
domination, 7, 9–11, 24, 30–31, 35–38, 40–45, 47–53, 57, 59, 72, 77–78, 84, 87–93, 105
Douglas, Kelly Brown, 32n32, 34n76

Eisenbaum, Pamela, 101, 112
enemy, 11, 15, 25–27, 40, 46, 48, 66, 68, 71, 77–78, 80–81, 86, 102–3; unlawful enemy combatant, 102, 104, 116n10

Filkins, Dexter, 46
Finkel, David, 88, 95n35, 95n56, 96n67, 107
full spectrum dominance, 10, 42–44, 46–47, 49–50, 53, 59, 98

Geneva Conventions, 47–48, 55n46, 116n10
global war on terror, 1, 3–4, 6–7, 9, 27, 31, 35–39, 41–42, 44, 46, 48–53, 57–58, 65, 83–86, 89–91, 103, 105

goodness and justice, 1–4, 6–7, 9–11, 17, 29, 31, 42, 49, 53, 57–59, 62, 72, 80, 82–83, 86–93, 97–107, 110, 112, 115–16
hatred, 2–3, 11, 27–29, 52, 58–59, 72, 87, 91, 99
Hedges, Chris, 44

ideology, 4–5, 7, 17, 22–26, 30, 36
insurgent/insurgency, 25, 46, 97, 102, 104, 107; counterinsurgency, 45–46
Iraq, 6, 9, 35, 37–39, 44–49, 51, 60, 65–66, 68–70, 84, 87–91, 97, 102, 107, 114
irony, 50–52, 118n49

justice. *See* goodness and justice
just war theory, 2, 10–11n5, 58, 69–71, 72n4, 90, 93, 96n64

Kinghorn, Warren, 65
King Jr., Martin Luther, 98–99
King, Stephen, 59
Kipling, Rudyard, 16

Lettini, Gabriella, 3, 74n25
Levinas, Emmanuel, 2, 11, 33n56, 97, 101, 103–6, 108–9, 111, 113–15, 116n1, 117n30
Litz, Brett, 10, 63–65, 91, 109–10
Lovecraft, H.P., 59

MacIntyre, Alisdair, 2, 11, 78–84, 86, 89–90, 93, 94n34
McLaughlin, John, 39
Meagher, Robert, 70–71
meaninglessness, 3, 11, 78, 84, 91–92, 97, 99
Moon, Zachary, 73n21
moral injury, 3–4, 10–11, 57–58, 60–68, 72, 77–79, 90–93, 97–98, 109–10; definition(s) of, 60–63, 66, 73n22, 77–78, 91, 93
morality, 4, 8, 10, 11, 27–30, 33, 36, 49, 53, 58–62, 64–65, 69–72, 78, 91, 97, 101–2, 106, 109, 111, 113; moral convention, 57–59, 61–69, 71–72, 77–79, 82–84, 86, 91–92; moral superiority, 49–50, 59, 62, 71, 98, 105
Morris, Errol, 40–41, 104

negative revelation, 3–4, 6–7, 10–11, 17, 42, 57–60, 72, 77–78, 90–93, 97–101, 106–9, 112, 115–16; definitions of, 57, 60, 72, 77, 99, 107–8, 116. *See also* revelation
Niebuhr, H. Richard, 5–6
Niebuhr, Reinhold, 50–52, 118n49
nomos, 66–68, 74n33
non-being, 17, 19–23
nothingness, 17–23
Nussbaum, Martha, 8, 60, 66–68, 74n33

Oath of Enlistment, 80, 94n15
O'Brien, Tim:7–8, 34n74, 57, 87, 91
Origen, 2, 57, 99

Powers, Kevin, 60, 78

Rambo, Shelly, 9, 112
revelation, 2–3, 5–7, 17, 41, 69, 84, 86, 98, 100–101, 105–6. *See also* negative revelation
Ricks, Thomas, 48
Rumsfeld, Donald, 10, 35–45, 47–51, 86, 104–5

Schleiermacher, Friedrich, 11, 13, 19, 108–11, 117n34, 118n49
Shay, Jonathan, 10, 62–64, 66–67, 74n33
Soldier's Creed, 81, 83, 86, 94n14
sovereignty, 10, 44–48, 50, 53, 59, 71, 98, 105
Stiltner, Brian, 61

telos, 82–84, 89–91, 93, 110
terrorist, 11, 25, 38, 47–48, 97
thémis, 62–63, 66, 74n33
Thomas Aquinas, 54n20

Tillich, Paul, 3, 9, 11, 14, 17, 19–24, 26, 29–31n4, 78
Tirman, John, 44
Tolkien, J.R.R., 31n7
totalitarian, 23–26, 30–31, 35
totality, 103–5, 109–10, 113
turning point (contrition), 51, 97–101, 108–12, 116, 118n49

Waggoner, Ed, 54
Walzer, Michael, 11n5, 69–71, 72n4, 96n64
weapons of mass destruction (WMD), 38–39, 47
Weil, Simone, 12n10, 72n2
Wiinikka-Lydon, Joseph, 66, 92

Yeterian, Julie D., 73n2

About the Author

Rev. Dr. Michael S. Yandell is senior minister at First Christian Church (Disciples of Christ), Greensboro, North Carolina. A graduate of Brite Divinity School, Michael completed a PhD in theological studies at Emory University in 2020, with a concentration in Religion, Conflict, and Peacebuilding. A U.S. Army veteran, he served as an enlisted explosive ordnance disposal (E.O.D.) specialist from 2002 to 2006. His recent publications on moral injury include "Do Not Torment Me: The Morally Injured Gerasene Demoniac" in *Moral Injury: A Guidebook for Understanding and Engagement*, edited by Brad E. Kelle (New York: Lexington Books, 2020); "Moral Injury and Human Relationship: A Conversation," *Pastoral Psychology*, 68, no. 1 (February 2019); "Hope in the Void," *Plough Quarterly*, no. 8 (Spring 2016); and "The War Within," *The Christian Century*, 132, no. 1 (January 7, 2015).

www.ingramcontent.com/pod-product-compliance
Lightning Source LLC
Chambersburg PA
CBHW020126010526
44115CB00008B/997